HOW TO MAKE A WRONG RELATIONSHIP RIGHT

HOW TO MAKE A WRONG RELATIONSHIP RIGHT

by
Dr. Sir Walter L. Mack Jr.

How to Make a Wrong Relationship Right
ISBN 978-1-936314-14-0
Copyright © 2010 Dr. Sir Walter L.Mack Jr.

Published by Word & Spirit Books
PO Box 701403
Tulsa,OK. 74170

Contents

DEDICATION

I would to dedicate this book to the churches that have allowed me to pastor and lead them in the effort of building relationships for Kingdom impact. First, I would like to thank Union Baptist Church in Winston-Salem, North Carolina, for being a tremendous ministry that understands the importance of relationships. You continue to teach me how important relationships are, and I am most blessed to be able to pastor you and grow with you. Thanks for all of your support. Stay committed to the work of making relationships right.

I would also like to thank the New Hope Granville Missionary Baptist Church in Oxford, North Carolina. Thank you for taking a chance on me by giving me my first opportunity to pastor. I want you to know that I still value the relationships that were established while you allowed me to lead you. Be blessed and remain commited to the work of building relationships.

Introduction

One of the greatest miracles God has ever provided for us is the miracle of relationships. Relationships are those inter- actions that we have with others that may affect our total understanding of how we interpret our world view. Relationships are critical because they allow us to enter into another person's reality, while at the same time, share our own reality. It is God's intention that we be in relationship with Him and with one another. It is quite interesting to me that the cross that Jesus died upon has a vertical extension and a horizontal extension. Symbolically, it could be that the vertical extension repre- sents Christ's relationship with God, and the horizontal extension represents His relationship with humanity. God desires us to be in relation- ship with Him and each other.

> *It is God's intention that we be in relationship with Him and with one another.*

Recently, I released the vision theme for our ministry as we seek to address matters of the kingdom, and that theme is: "Building Relationships: Establishing the New, and Reclaiming the Old." The mysticism behind this theme is that there comes a time when the ministry needs to focus on literally *making* relationships. That means there needs to be intentional effort on behalf of the members to meet new people, speak to new people, and get to know new people. That is establishing the new. Reclaiming the old involves reaching back and restoring relationships that have been broken, distorted, or lost. Relationships are primary and fundamental for ministry fulfillment.

Dean of Preachers, Dr. Gardner Calvin Taylor, in his most impressive preaching pressed the claim for relationships when he stated, "When we move into moral and spiritual considerations we act as if we are on our own. So many of us tend to think that we have things exclusively in our hand. What we do is our business; nobody has anything to do with it. Yes, this is the philosophy of our generation, and our neuroses and psychoses run away with us, our nerves crack, our jails are full, our marriages are hardly more in number than our divorces, and our liquor and drug bills soar. Everywhere people are wringing their hands. Thugs mug, legislatures steal and rob, business executives plunder, and we wonder why. What has happened? What has gone wrong?"[1] Well, one problem is that relationships are no longer in place to keep us grounded and accountable to somebody else other than ourselves. Relationships are

Relationships are important, they are significant, and they do have a place in the establishment of the kingdom.

important, they are significant, and they do have a place in the establishment of the kingdom.

In the development of any relationship, I discovered that there are three positions into which every relationship will fit:

1) Pre-Relationship

2) Practicing Relationship

3) Post-Relationship

Pre-Relationship is the position that people exist in before you encounter them. In the pre-relationship position, a person is accumulating experiences, history, and encounters before they meet you, which will impact how they present themselves when they do meet you.

A relationship has reached the Practicing Relationship position when you actually meet people and the contact substantiates either a one-time experience or a long-term experience. It is in a practicing relationship, that what a person has gone through in their *Pre-* affects you, by how that person now relates to you in the *Practicing*. It is ideal that relationships remain practicing, and most good relationships do. However, there are times when relationships move to the Post-Relationship position.

Post-Relationships are those relationships that we move away from, that are no longer a part of our lives. Post-relationships are shaped by those people who were in our lives for a season, and while they were there, they made deposits into us, but now they are gone. Regardless of what position the relationships are in your life, it is a good thing to value them and learn from them.

I recall a story that I read in an English class while attending Elon College in North Carolina, which speaks directly to the value of relationships. As the story evolves, it reveals the innermost self-absorption of an individual who had a selfish desire to separate himself from the world he knew—from his family who loved him and the friends who were pivotal beings in his life.

The man in the story had a desire to build a house on an island where he could isolate himself away from everyone. So he told his wife and his children that he was leaving them forever, and that he was going to live in seclusion. After he arrived on the island, he immediately began to build a house. It took him several weeks, and the entire time that he was feverishly working, he was also gloating over the fact that this would be "his house" where he could be aloof and live in solitude.

Finally, after working expeditiously by himself, it came time to put the last nail in the house. Resiliently, he climbed the ladder and began to drive the last nail into the house. However, it was while he was up on the ladder hammering the last nail that he made a mistake and accidently nailed his hand to the plank on the wall. The pain was so excruciating that while standing high on the ladder, he accidently dropped the hammer. With the hammer laying on the floor and his hand stuck to the wall, it became evident to the man that he was all alone, and he immediately realized that there was no one else in sight to rescue him from this desolate situation. It was only then that the man discovered the necessity for "relationship." Sadly, at this point, the likelihood of someone coming to rescue him was literally nonexistent. Through his vain self-discovery, he ultimately realized it is not only ludicrous to live alone on an island, but it is even more ridiculous avoiding relationships with others.

This story speaks so eloquently to the need for relationships. But perhaps more significant is our need from time to time to make a wrong relationships right. *How To Make a Wrong Relationship Right*, is a reading that will inspire you to take an introspective look at the many relationships in which we find ourselves. To say that a relationship is "wrong" does not necessarily mean that the relationship at its inception was wrong, but by the time misunderstandings happen, miscommunications take place, or insecurities set in, even in the best of relationships, wrong things begin to happen. Because of the pivotal investments we make in certain relationships such as years, time, money, and experiences, there are times we just don't want to walk away from the relationship. Therefore, the question that rings out loudly in our minds is, *How do we make this right?* How do we correct the problems of relationships, how do we discern if they are correctable, and what do we do once the issues are corrected? How do we walk away if we discover that the issues are not correctable? These are difficult relationship questions, and there are no easy relationship answers.

Even in the best of relationships, wrong things begin to happen.

The uniqueness of this reading is that it encompasses a variety of relationships which include spiritual, leadership, business, soul-mating, social networking, and love, just to name a few. It is vital that you get a clear understanding of the complexities of these individual relationships, because often what happens in one relationship of your life can have a domino effect on another relationship in which you are involved.

The scandal surrounding golf protégé Tiger Woods exemplifies the difficulties encountered in attempting to make a wrong relationship, right. This is, by far, one of the most popular stories that we have seen publicized in quite some time. Tiger Woods, the premier golfer in the world, icon for many of his fans, role model for many youth, and positive endorser for mainline products, was caught in a web of infidelity, which entailed several illicit sexual relationships. This scandal shocked the world because there had been an idealized image portrayed by the media of Tiger prior to these shocking revelations, which was unrealistic.

This unfortunate situation affected every other relationship that meant something to Tiger. Not only did this humiliation affect Woods' marital relationship, but it also affected his professional, social, and even his spiritual relationships. Tiger Woods' "secret world" was now plastered on the television, Internet, and world magazines. He was caught.

For months it was said that Tiger's public relations experts dealt with the issue for Tiger, wrestling with such questions as, "How do we make this right? How do we take the wrong that Tiger did, and find a ray of hope in it? How do we convince people that Tiger is a better person as a result of dealing with some very obviously foolish mistakes?" These questions had to be raised as Tiger suffered the loss of family, friends, endorsements, and mentees, all of the relationships that were significant to him. The solution the public relations experts came up with was this: "Let's rely on the relationship that Tiger had with his Father."

A commercial was produced using the genius of technology showing Tiger Woods being lectured by his father. Even though his father was dead, a previous recording of his father's voice projected clearly asking questions like, "Tiger what are you thinking, how are you feeling, and what are you going to do differently?" Creatively, they took that interview from years past and made it come alive for Tiger's situation today. All of this was done to save and recover some relationships for "ole" Tiger.

The jury is still out on whether Tiger's situation can be resolved, but the lesson to be learned here is that almost every action that we do affects other relationships in our lives. Not intentionally meaning to hurt others and certainly not looking to be hurt, we find ourselves wondering what it is that we need to do to make relationships right, get things straight, find some solace, or reconcile with peace.

This was also the reality in the life of King David. David had many relationships in his life that, in some ways, were webbed together. This book unfolds many of those relationships that

David found himself in, as well as the impact they had upon him. It will also reveal how he navigated these relationships while seeking to fulfill his destiny. Though David was a man after God's own heart, on an even greater level, the real story of David includes the ambivalent mistakes made in his many relationships. It is more important for us that we not only see where he made those mistakes, but we also see where David sought to make these damaged relationships right. This is our challenge, because in every relationship mistakes will be made, whether you commit them or whether they are conferred upon you, and the prevailing question is "How do we make it right?" Making a wrong relationship right does not always mean you stay until something different is done. Sometimes making the relationship right means removing yourself from the relationship, or it could mean you stay in the relationship until it is made right. There is a time for all considerations, but this reading will help you know and discern which decision may be right for you.

The prevailing question is "How do we make it right?"

The most effective way to read this book is to not sit in judgment about David and the decisions that he made concerning his relationships, but consider your own interactions and the things that you need to do, in order to become a better you. Read and learn how to make a wrong relationship right.

CHAPTER 1

MAKING A WRONG
Spiritual Relationship Right

*David mustered the pick of the troops of Israel—thirty
divisions of them. Together with his soldiers, David headed
for Baalah to recover the Chest of God, which was called by
the Name God-of-the-Angel-Armies, who was enthroned
over the pair of angels on the Chest.*

*They placed the Chest of God on a brand-new oxcart and
removed it from Abinadab's house on the hill. Uzzah and
Ahio, Abinadab's sons, were driving the new cart loaded
with the Chest of God, Ahio in the lead and Uzzah alongside the Chest. David and the whole company of Israel were
in the parade, singing at the top of their lungs and playing
mandolins, harps, tambourines, castanets, and cymbals.
When they came to the threshing floor of Nacon, the oxen
stumbled, so Uzzah reached out and grabbed the Chest of
God. God blazed in anger against Uzzah and struck him
hard because he had profaned the Chest. Uzzah died on the
spot, right alongside the Chest.*

2 Samuel 6:1-7 MSG

If there is ever going to be any validity to the relationship(s) that you seek to establish, it is important for you to know that it is the Spirit who ultimately makes the difference. Every relationship must be rooted in the Spirit of God, especially if it is going to possess the strength and depth that is needed to withstand all of the inconveniences, changes, interruptions, skepticisms, gossip, and all of the conditions that inadvertently reside in any relationship. A spiritual relationship is a God-centered one that encompasses purity, power, and shows its effectiveness for the purpose that God establishes. If this is not understood, a relationship can become ineffective and lead to a toxic disposition which creates more hurt than love, more darkness than light, more fear than faith, and more criticism than compliment. Therefore, the effectiveness of any relationship has to hinge on a spiritual undergirding, that shall construe and stabilize it through good times and bad times.

Above all, your relationship with God must be most important.

Above all, your relationship with God must be most important and must supersede all other associations. Whether it is a platonic, business, or a romantic relationship, it is important to make certain that God is in the mix. If God is not primary, and does not serve as the foundation for each union, then the relationship is missing the component that is crucial for creating a cohesive bond that will hold fast through any test and moment of trial.

In 2 Samuel 6:1-7, we see an instance where David encountered a wrong spiritual relationship that he had to make right. Throughout the life of David, it is apparent that he was clear about his expected relationship with God. He had been anointed by Samuel, and chosen from among his brothers to be the next king of Israel, thus his assignment was focused and clear. Accordingly, in 2 Samuel 6:1, David has in his presence the Ark of the Covenant. This was a monumental advantage for David, because it was believed that wherever the Ark of the Covenant was, that was where the presence of God also abided.

The Ark of the Covenant was a wooden rectangular box made from acacia wood, which measured 2½ cubits long, 1½ cubits wide and 1½ cubits high (3 ¾ feet by 2 ¼ feet by 2 ¼ feet). It was covered with gold, and the box was to be transported by poles being inserted in rings at the four lower corners. On the top of the Ark was the covering called the mercy seat which was laced in gold and surrounded by two cherubs with their wings spread upward. (See Exodus 25:10-22.)

In this instance, David is transporting the Ark primarily for three reasons. First, the Ark was being transported because David felt a responsibility to God because He had protected him from the cruel and mean hand of Saul. Secondly, David is transporting the Ark because of a political obligation. David wanted Israel to worship in one place, and that one place would be Jerusalem. So he was transporting the Ark from Kirjeth-Jareem to Jerusalem to unify the worship of Israel.

Thirdly, he was transporting the Ark to protect it from the House of Saul—his chief enemy.

David's motive for transporting the Ark was good; however, the error arose in his choice of method for transport. David assigned Ahio, the son of Abinadab, to be in front of the Ark, and Uzzah, who was a very close friend to David, was assigned to travel behind the Ark. David also called an additional 30,000 foot soldiers to journey with the Ark to Jerusalem. But in the midst of their travel, tragedy occurs, and the Ark slips from the cart. Uzzah catches it before it falls, and though the Ark is spared, Uzzah dies. The death of Uzzah was inevitable because there was a covenant decree that if human hands ever touched the Ark, then death would come upon the subject.

It was the death of Uzzah that impeded the relationship that David had with God. When Uzzah died, David became so angry with God that he decided to leave the Ark at Obed-Edom's house. It was as though he believed that if he could leave the Ark, he could also leave God. Consequently, it is when he leaves the Ark, that David loses his joy, his peace, and his serenity. Fortunately for David, God's presence extends beyond the Ark, because God is everywhere.

He limited God's presence to that one symbolic image.

God Is Omnipresent

The problem with David's relationship as concerns the Ark of the Covenant is that he limited God's presence to that one symbolic image. Unquestionably, God is omnipresent, and because He is everywhere at the same time, He is not limited to the confines of space and time. All of this means that His presence transcends the places we occupy, signifying that we don't have the power to leave God anywhere, but yet we can find God everywhere. David forgot this important fact, and as a result, his relationship with God became impaired because of his diminished view of what the actual presence of God meant verses the symbolism of the Ark of the Covenant.

There are times when we are just like David, when we encounter situations when we become fixated on people, places, and things, and have a stronger relationship with these things than we have with God. In the same way, there is a danger when you have stronger relationship with the physical church building, than you do with God. It is problematic when you have a closer relationship with people than you do with God. To add impact to injury, when these individuals mistreat you, deny or even deceive you, it is ultimately your relationship with God that suffers… not the people who hurt you.

In the church, people are often hurt because of relationships that may go wrong. Perhaps you have been in a church relationship where you shared your inner most thoughts with someone about your weakness or your temptations, only to discover that your secrets were shared among uncaring people in that congregation. Perhaps you are someone who depended on the church to be there when you lost your job, your parent, your child, and you were looking for the church to respond with love and kindness. Instead, you found nothing but cold-ness and a blatant show of disregard toward your pain and suf-fering. Maybe you have been in a church relationship where you have been exploited, abused, or simply misunderstood. Whichever is the case, it is important that you make a dis-tinction between the church of God, and the God of the church. Essentially, God existed before the church building, and God will be there after the church building is gone.

This truth became apparent to me when I was just a young boy, and my father's church burned to the ground. Of course this fire was a great tragedy and because of it, we would even-tually have to relocate about 750 people who now had no place to worship. Nevertheless, I remember very vividly how my father handled the situation. One minister called and said to my father, "I am sorry to hear that you no longer have a church, and that your church burned down."

My father's response to that minister was simply this, "Thank you for your concern, but I must correct you. The Church didn't burn, the building did. And the only thing that's on fire with my Church, is the fire that's burning inside of us. Though we don't have a building, come Sunday we will have Church." That faithful group of people met the Sunday following the fire at a funeral home, and on that morning, the fire of God's Spirit was burning so, that the people almost forgot that their church building no longer stood.

I believe I cannot stress enough the point of difference between connecting with the church building versus connecting with God. My father's congregation keenly separated the building from what really made them the "Church." They understood that the real Church was not a building, (not the Ark of the Covenant), but their church was their relationship, bond, trust in God and each other. This is so critical because any relationship has the potential for hurt and disappointment, but when your relationship is firm with God, He will give an assurance that you can totally trust and depend on Him. Furthermore, He will even give you a greater understanding about the hurt and disappointment which you encountered.

How Do We Establish a Right Relationship with God?

A RIGHT RELATIONSHIP WITH GOD BEGINS WITH A RIGHT CONFESSION OF GOD

A right relationship with God begins with a right confession. Your confession for a right relationship begins when you confess Christ as your Savior. A great definition of Confessional Faith can be found in Romans 10:8-11 NIV:

> *But what does it say? "The word is near you; it is in your mouth and in your heart," that is, the word of faith we are proclaiming: That if you confess with your mouth, "Jesus is Lord," and believe in your heart that God raised him from the dead, you will be saved. For it is with your heart that you believe and are justified, and it is with your mouth that you confess and are saved.*

As the Scripture says, "Anyone who trusts in him will never be put to shame."

If a relationship is to be established with God through Christ, one must confess Christ.

According to this scripture, if a relationship is to be established with God through Christ, one must confess Christ. So many times we establish a wrong relationship with God, because we believe that our relationship with God must begin with confessing our faults, short comings, our many sins, and so on. On the contrary, our sin is something that we have committed out of our humanity. It is rooted to our innate ability, which does not have the capability to save us. So why should we confess someone or something that does not have the ability to save us? You cannot save you; therefore your relationship with God must begin with a confession from your mouth, not about yourself, but about God, who can save. Such confession must pertain to a belief in your heart, that God raised a dead Man, and gave Him all power in His hand.

Jesus became like us that we should become more like Him to strengthen our relationship with God. Gregory of Nazianzus once noted the many contradictions in the life of Christ. He noted that The Bread of Life started His ministry by being hungry. The Living Water ended His earthly ministry by being thirsty. The One who said He could give us rest, also said that He had nowhere to lay His head. Though He was accused of having a demon, He spent most of His time casting out demons. The One who wept, also is the One who wipes tears from our eyes. The Jesus who was sold for thirty pieces of silver, ended up redeeming the whole world. The One who was brought as a lamb to be slain, was also the One who called himself the Good Shepherd. Though Jesus died, it was His death that destroyed death.[1] This revelation of Christ is so powerful because while it shows His humanity, it also shows His divinity. Our relationship with Him is rooted in His passion to identify with us by feeling what we feel, and going through what we go through. It was the desire of Christ to be like us, that we may eventually be like Him.

If confession is done properly, everyone who is connected with you will know that you confess Jesus as your Savior. This is critical when you are developing a relationship with others, because you want people to know that Christ is your priority. If your confession of Christ extends beyond the realm of something that you only do in church, and it becomes clearly apparent in your everyday life, then others will not feel comfortable with drinking around you, swearing, or even mentioning their corrupt behaviors. Everybody connected to you will understand that you unapologetically confess Christ.

A RELATIONSHIP WITH GOD BEGINS WITH A RIGHT POSSESSION OF FAITH

It is one thing to confess God, but it is another thing to possess God. Possession, in this case, is not the sense of having sole ownership, because God is free to all. But possession is viewed as the way of making your faith personal to you. One of the most fascinating scenarios of faith building a relationship is found in Luke 8:43-48 with the woman who was suffering from an issue of blood. As Jesus was passing through an area, in the crowd that day there was a woman who, for twelve years, had been afflicted with hemorrhages. She had spent every penny she had on doctors but not one had been able to help her. She slipped in from behind and touched the edge of Jesus' robe. Jesus said, *"Daughter, you took a risk trusting me, and now you're healed and whole. Live well, live blessed!"* (Luke 8:48 MSG).

In the opening part of that scripture passage, the woman is only identified as a *certain woman*. But after she activated her faith and reached out and touched the hem of Jesus' garment, the Bible declares that she was made whole. Then this woman began to thank Jesus, and Jesus said to her, *Daughter* it was not I that made you whole, but it was your faith. Most of the time we celebrate the woman's healing, but here I would like to recognize the induction of her daughtership. Jesus moves her from a "certain woman" to the position of "daughter." It is apparent to me that the only thing that solidified her relationship with Christ, was the fact that she possessed faith.

Things may not be visible to your eyes, that does not mean that faith can't see them.

A.W. Tozer declared that "Faith sees the invisible, but it does not see the non-existent."[2] Though things may not be visible to your eyes, that does not mean that faith can't see them. Benjamin Mays said this about faith, "It must be borne in mind that the tragedy of life doesn't lie in not reaching your goal. The tragedy is having no goal to reach. It is not a calamity to die with dreams unfulfilled, but it is calamity not to dream. It is not a disaster to be unable to capture your ideal, but it is a disaster to have no ideal to capture. It is not a disgrace not to reach the stars, but it is a disgrace to have no stars to reach for. Not failure but low aim is sin."[3] This woman in Luke 8 reached her goal—she dreamed of a healing, captured the moment, and reached out and connected with the hem of Jesus.

It is your faith that becomes the connector for your relationship with God. Your faith is the bridge to get you to God, your faith is the signal that God recognizes to let Him know that you confess Him and you possess Him. Romans 5:1-2 phrases it this way: *Therefore, since we have been justified through faith, we have peace with God through our Lord Jesus Christ, through whom we have gained access by faith into this grace in which we stand. And we rejoice in hope of the glory of God* (NIV).

A RELATIONSHIP WITH GOD BEGINS WITH A RIGHT EXPERIENCE WITH GOD

There are times when God will prove your relationship with Him through various experiences that you will have in this life. There are many people who did not come to know God and develop a relationship with God through an experience in church or by the approach of some convincing evangelistic minister, but there are those who find the Lord while in the midst of trouble and trial. Some have found the Lord while bullets were flying over their head, while people were over in a corner near them putting drugs in their body, while a brawl was taking place in another section of the nightclub. Some experiences are permitted by God to lead you directly to Him. Why did God permit you to go through that bad relationship, get fired from the job, experience that bad separation or divorce, or have an attack come against your name or character? Could it be that God orchestrated it because He already knows that blessed are those who are persecuted for His Name's sake? (Matthew 5:11.) Could it be because God knows how to work all things together for good? (Romans 8:28.)

Some time ago, there was story on national news about a young lady in Kansas City who allegedly had a bad spat with her boyfriend, to the point where she decided to end the relationship. In the midst of the couple's confrontation, the story reported that the boyfriend took out a gun, and began shooting at the young lady's car. A bullet went through the car, and ended up in her head. This story made headline news because the bullet never cracked her skin, never touched her skull, nor did it touch her brain. Why? Because miraculously enough, the bullet was caught in this young lady's hair. Apparently the woman had weave in her hair, which is no more than synthetic hair mixed in with one's own hair. It was the weave that caught the bullet, and spared the life of this young lady. Maybe this woman thought that her last hair appointment with her beautician was just another appointment, but what she didn't realize is that God would use the style she wore and the thickness of her hair to save her life. In the words of a preacher by the name of Freddie Haynes, "God is 'unbe-weavable.'"

Your faith in God is more significant than any person, place, or thing that you can possess.

Now the news organizations did not say if this young lady had a relationship with God or not, but if my life had been spared like that, you could not stop me from having a right relationship with God. That is certainly where my faith would lie, not in people, places, or things, but in the God who saved me. That is having a right relationship with God.

How to Make a Wrong Spiritual Relationship Right

Making a wrong spiritual relationship right means that you refuse to be like David, who put his faith in material things when God is spiritual. Realize that your faith in God is more significant than any person, place, or thing that you can possess. Do not limit God to any one place, God is omnipresent and God has the ability to be everywhere at the same time. Making a wrong spiritual relationship right does not begin with anyone else, it begins with you and the relationship that you have with God.

While there are many benefits from having a right relationship with God, none surpasses the benefit of having peace in knowing that your soul is connected to Him. Henri Nouwen in his book, *Sabattical Journey*, decribes a relationship between a high wire circus "flyer" and "catcher." "The flyer lets go of the trapeze and flies high above the audience in moments of frightening danger. One of the Flying Roudellas said, 'The flyer must never try to catch the catcher. The flyer just trusts that catcher will catch.'"[4] So it is with our relationship with God, it is our job to let go and fly through life, fly through trials, fly through trouble and tribulations, and trust that when we let go, it is God who will catch us.

SPIRITUAL RELATIONSHIP
REFLECTION QUESTIONS

1. Do you spend time with God daily in prayer, meditation, and scripture reading? Do you create your own time for personal worship?

2. Can you recall a time that you sensed God doing something in your life that later was confirmed by the results?

3. A wise woman once told me, "Never love anything that does not have the capacity to love you back. Don't love cars, watches, clothes, and money. Love God and people who have the capacity to love you back." Have you ever been guilty of loving something or someone more than you loved God? If so, when did you discover this error, and what did it take for you to correct it?

4. What are the things you need to do to work on your spiritual relationship with God, family, and others?

5. In your own spiritual walk, have you ever had an unhealthy relationship with church? How did this relationship hinder your growth in God?

6. What advice would you give to people who are seeking a deeper relationship with God and the church?

CHAPTER 2

MAKING A WRONG
Leadership Relationship Right

He came to some sheep pens along the road. There was a cave there and Saul went in to relieve himself. David and his men were huddled far back in the same cave. David's men whispered to him, "Can you believe it? This is the day GOD was talking about when he said, 'I'll put your enemy in your hands. You can do whatever you want with him.'" Quiet as a cat, David crept up and cut off a piece of Saul's royal robe. Immediately, he felt guilty. He said to his men, "GOD forbid that I should have done this to my master, GOD's anointed, that I should so much as raise a finger against him. He's GOD's anointed!" David held his men in check with these words and wouldn't let them pounce on Saul. Saul got up, left the cave, and went on down the road.

1 Samuel 24:3-7 MSG

David found solace in having a relationship with God because he had not always had the best relationships to surface in his life. A case in point would be the relationship he had with his enemy Saul. In this chapter, we will discuss the emotional, psychological, and spiritual trauma that one may experience being under the authority of a toxic and venomous leader like Saul.

There are many people today who are living under the weight of spiritual abuse and do not know how to address it because of their respect for the very leader who is abusing them. We will discover how David showed his loyalty to Saul, how he did everything he could to mend the relationship, but more importantly we will see how he maintained his own relationship with God in the midst of turmoil.

David had many interesting experiences with relationships in his life, and one of those experiences occurred within the relationship that he had with Saul. Saul was selected to be the king of Israel, not by God but by the people. In 1 Samuel chapters 9 and 10, Saul is introduced as a handsome and rather tall son of a wealthy Benjamite named Kish. One day while searching for his father's donkeys, Saul stumbles into a village in the Ephramite hills seeking a word from a local seer. Unbeknownst to Saul, the seer he was seeking was none other than the prophet Samuel. It is Samuel who then anoints Saul as king. Later Saul was acclaimed king by the people. (1 Samuel 9:1-14; 10:1,17-27.) To seal his kingship among the people, Saul defeated the Ammonites in a vicious fight, and the people were now made confident in the leadership of their new king. (1 Samuel 11.)

While many believe the biblical account of the institution of kingship inspires a certain level of suspicion, God actually intended for the office of the King to function under the auspices of His leadership as given through the prophet. Therefore, Saul was doing good as long as he following the instructions of God dictated by way of the prophet. It is when Saul refused to listen to the voice of Samuel, that God fired Saul and told Samuel to go to Bethlehem and find a new king whose name was David.

Samuel goes to the house of Jesse and is directed by God to select David because of his heart. Samuel then anoints David to be next king of Israel. What is interesting is that Saul's anointing for leadership was validated by the people, but David's anointing for leadership was validated by God. This is where David had to face his first test of leadership. When David was anointed to be king, Saul still occupied the position. This meant that David had to live with having the number one anointing, while occupying the number two position. In other words, Saul would be serving as the president of the company with no qualifications (no anointing), while David served as the vice-president with all of the qualifications (the anointing). Consequently, David had to remain loyal to the one with no qualifications until God saw fit to strip Saul of his position.

How did David do this? How did David exist under leadership that was not only defunct, but also out to destroy him and completely take him out of commission before the people

How could David function under leadership that had become toxic?

of Israel? How did David exist knowing that his anointing was under attack, and that his gifts were being denied over the simple theory of jealousy? How did David deal with the rumors and character insults perpetuated from the lips of Saul because he had become cynical of David's popularity among the women of the day, and even envious of his military prowess? How could David function under leadership that had become toxic to others around him, that introduced a spirit of suspicion about him in the minds of people who would potentially support David?

If we can look at how David existed under this kind of nefarious leadership, then maybe we can discern a plan for those of you who have to live under leadership that is supporting you on the outside, but is destroying you on the inside. There are many people who are living their lives in silence because they do not know how to speak out and voice all of the hurt and pain that they deal with from the leader that they have been assigned to serve.

Recently, we as a nation had to witness the death of two people who had ascribed their faith to a positive thinking/spiritual direction leader. In the midst of this group of people seeking to cleanse themselves from the demons that were in them by sweating out their demons and all of their spiritual impurities were two people who died in this ritual.

While I do not want to debate the real reason and the real cause of death for these individuals, it is apparent that they had ascribed themselves to a leader that they trusted and believed that if they did what he said, that they could sweat out whatever demon they had in them. The one they had trusted led them into behaviors that cost them their lives.

We see this kind of thing happen not only in spiritual circles, but also in political circles where it seems more and more governors, congressmen, and senators are resigning because of character and ethical lapses. We citizens are more and more forced to ascribe to leadership that is less than honorable. It seems that it is becoming more and more popular for teachers to have affairs with their students, police officers are getting caught and fired for being undercover drug users/dealers, not to mention the sports figures and rap artists who are providing such a poor form of leadership to our youth that mimic them, and even desire deeply to be like them. It is apparent that in many ways, there is a crisis in leadership relationships.

Howard Gardner says that, "A leader is an individual who significantly affects the thoughts, feelings, and /or behaviors of a significant number of individuals."[1] While this may be true, leadership often brings with it numerous chances of risk and non-popularity. Leadership is not easy by any stretch of the imagination. It involves chance, risk, uncertainty, all hinging on what you believe to be the right thing to do.

Heifetz and Linsky in their book, *Leadership On the Line* say, "To lead is to live dangerously because when leadership counts, when you lead people through difficult change, you challenge what people hold dear—their daily habits, tools, loyalties, and ways of thinking—with nothing more to offer perhaps than a possibility. Moreover, leadership often means exceeding the authority you are given to tackle the challenge at hand."[2] When leadership is done right it is a great thing, however when it is done with private agendas and toxic behaviors it can have a very negative effect on the relationships that form as a result.

There are many people who have a relationship with bad leadership and don't even know it. Consider the various toxic leadership styles that we must learn how to relate to if we are going to be effective in building relationships.

The Non-Visionary Leader

Only five percent of pastors ever come up with new ideas, concepts or observations.

The non-visionary leader is the leader who has high expectations for your performance, but does not give you the necessary tools, training, information, and knowledge for you to do what is requested. C. Peter Wagner, researcher and statistician for the church culture, observed that that only five percent of pastors ever come up with new ideas, concepts or observations. Another 15 percent of pastors are what he calls "innovators," which means they are innovative enough to follow the template of ideas demonstrated by the five percent who create great ideas in ministry. This leaves 80% of pastors in the category Wagner calls "programmatic." This group rarely comes up with anything new to do in ministry, and as a matter of fact, if something is suggested, they need very detailed steps to actually implement what has been placed before them.[3]

These are striking numbers especially when you think of the numbers of parishioners in churches who are sitting under leadership and yet only five percent of their leaders truly have a vision. If the leader doesn't have a vision, then it is almost impossible for them to work the vision, yet they hold a position and a title where this is supposed to be the job. The non-visionary leader can drive his parishioners crazy with ideas, thoughts, emotional responses, and even dreams, but fails to have a vision on how to bring it to pass.

The Disrespectful Leader

The disrespectful leader has an obnoxious, arrogant, narcissistic, and over bearing disposition. This leader does not have any regard for personal time and space, but will often impose upon your rights for the sake of a paycheck, promotion, or preaching opportunity. This leader does not do well with the answer "no," and believes that their opinion should be your opinion. The disrespectful leader equates *power* with *rights*. If you have little power then

> *The disrespectful leader equates power with rights.*

you have little right. There is no such thing as a system; the only thing that exist is their way. How can you have a relationship with a disrespectful leader?

The Overly Critical Leader

The overly critical leader is one who is not pleased with anything.

The overly critical leader is one who is not pleased with anything. It doesn't matter what the task or goal is, the overly critical leader will find a fault or present questions that are often times more cynical than they are useful. This leader is often a perfectionist, and anything less than their standard is subject to criticism. The overly critical leader is difficult to please, and if they are pleased, often times it is because they or someone that they personally endorse, performs the task. The overly critical leader is dangerous because they have the charisma and the capacity to persuade others that they ought to be overly critical towards you, too. How can you have a relationship with an overly critical leader?

The Insecure Leader

The insecure leader is a leader who lacks self-confidence, a healthy perception of themselves, and true knowledge of who they are. Because of this, the insecure leader will often project their deep inner thoughts and emotions about themselves onto you. For example, the insecure leader may often say demeaning things to you, because deep down inside they are not pleased with themselves. Insecure leaders watch their positions like a hawk watches meat, because in their mind there is somebody always after what they have. Do not be surprised when you hear the insecure leader tearing other people down to lift up himself. This is how such leaders survive and make you think they are very effective. How can you have a relationship with an insecure leader?

The insecure leader will often project their deep inner thoughts and emotions about themselves onto you.

The Non-Appreciative Leader

The number one complaint many employees have of their supervisors is that they work for a leader who does not appreciate the essence of who they are. The non-appreciative leader will see your responsibility as "your" responsibility, and will tell you, "Because I pay you, I don't have to appreciate you." This is the leader who will never say words like, "thank you," "this is great work," "you didn't have to do this," or "what can I do to make things better for you". The non-appreciative leader doesn't appreciate, because in their mind they have the idea that you owe them something and if you don't produce, they just merely move on to the next person who will. In a sense, they refuse to appreciate you because to appreciate you will take the lime light off of the things they do, and the things that they

They refuse to appreciate you because to appreciate you will take the lime light off of the things they do.

make happen. How can you have a relationship with a non-appreciative leader?

The Abusive/Harassing Leader

This is probably the most destructive leadership style of them all, simply because this leadership motive is centered around power and authority. This abusive style of leadership often manifests itself through hurtful words, fear tactics, threats and punishment, not to mention the force of physical contact that is often uninvited and certainly a violation of your personal space. This leader is solely about what you can do for them, and often times it has nothing to do with the job, but it is personal joy and pleasure that they are seeking. They are empowered when they can control you, and will remind you of your helplessness if you seek to come against them. How can you have a relationship with an abusive/harassing leader?

The Destructive Leader

The destructive leader is so mean that they will even sabotage their own work to create a need for you to need them. The destructive leader lives in confusion; they love to tear down character, reputations, and any plan that is not theirs. The destructive leader spends more time finding ways to undo things, rather than putting things together. They are destructive, and in some ways most dangerous, because this kind of leader often gets others to do their dirty work and will turn others against you to prove themselves to be strong and right.

The destructive leader lives in confusion.

How can you have a relationship with a destructive leader?

If you are someone who is existing in a leadership-relationship that is toxic and not healthy, then it is vital for you to know what it is you need to do to make a wrong relationship right. It is important that you understand your place is to always be respectful and dutiful to your task, as long as it does not require you to compromise your character and integrity. Dr. Walter Fluker in his book, *Ethical Leadership*, gives us four primary components we can turn to to make a wrong leadership relationship, right: Integrity, Empathy, Hope, and Security.

Make a Wrong Leadership Relationship Right with Integrity

The Chinese symbol for integrity is *Te*. While this could also mean inherent virtue and goodness, the best interpretation for this is character implies that it comes straight from the heart.[4] Thus integrity is that which comes straight from the heart. Your integrity is important because it informs your actions and behaviors, including how you respond to less than honorable leadership. Whenever there is lack of integrity in leadership, you can help bring correction to this area by being determined to be full of integrity yourself while also being respectful. Your integrity will inform your choices, direction, and will help to regulate your emotions.

Howard G. Hendricks reminded leaders of the importance of integrity when he stated, "Vision without integrity is not mission—it's manipulation."[5] It is important to note that integrity and character must become the foundation and basis for making a wrong leadership relationship right. Just because your personal Saul is out to destroy you, does not mean that you have to be on a mission to destroy him/her. You must remain dutiful to your responsibility as long as it does not violate your right to have personal peace and serenity in your own life. Lord Macauley declared, "The measure of a man's character is what he would do if he knew he would never be found out. Character is what you are in the dark, and reputation is only what others believe you to be."[6] Throughout all of Saul's tactics to destroy him, David's integrity did not allow him to destroy Saul even when he had the opportunity to do so. Even though living under bad leadership is very trying, learn how to abide in peace until God relocates you in His own time.

Make a Wrong Leadership Relationship Right with Empathy

While integrity is more about behavior, empathy is more about emotions. The reason that you must possess empathy is because empathy has a way of putting you in the place of others. There is an old adage that says, "Hurting people often hurt people." If you are under destructive leadership, there is nothing wrong with you requesting a meeting or a conversation over coffee and a bagel, to seek to get to the bottom of why your leader has the attitude that they have toward you and what it is you can do to help facilitate a more wholesome relationship.

Even though David was aware that Saul was trying to take his life, never forget that David would often play the harp for Saul to sooth his evil spirit. Empathy has a way of making you go over and beyond the call of duty to try to make the relationship work, doing what you need to do until God delivers. David played the harp for Saul, saturating his ears with the sound of music that sprung from the passion inside of him, moving his fingers to pull gently on the strings. David did this even when he knew Saul was out to kill him.

Not only was David moved to play for Saul to soothe his spirit, but David's empathy even moved him to save Saul's life. It was in a cave one day when Saul was relieving himself that David came behind and could have killed him. But the empathy of David did not allow his knife to stab Saul in the back while he was using the restroom. David just cut off a piece of Saul's garment and later showed it to him as if to say, "If I wanted to kill you I could have, but it was my empathy that spared you."

You might be in position to destroy your leader with what you have seen and what you know, but remember that you will be in the number one position one day, and what goes around, comes around.

Make a Wrong Leadership Relationship Right with Hope

Nothing can hinder your creativity and diminish your optimism like working under leadership that refuses to follow proper protocol to do things the right way. However, regardless of the refusals to follow protocol and the lack of responsibility that the leader you serve under may have, never give up hope for them to make a change.

Hope is not just a concept, but hope is an action.

James Gustafson describes hope as confidence in our future. He stated, "Hope is carried by confidence that life is more reliable than unreliable, that the future is open, that new possibilities of life exist."[7] This must be the reality that every relationship mender must hold on to. Hope is not just a concept, but hope is an action. Anybody who is serious about confronting the despair that irresponsibile leaders bring, must understand that hope is not just being optimistic or having a positive outlook on the situation, but hope is rooted in the faith that says even when things don't look quite optimistic, we can still have hope. Hebrews 11:1

says, *Now faith is the substance of things hoped for, the evidence of things not seen* (NKJV). Before any radical transformation is to happen in the lives of people who present bad leadership, the ones who are affected by the leadership must have hope that they can change. It is your job to pray for that to happen.

Make a Wrong Relationship Right with Security

It is vital for anyone who is seeking to fix a relationship that is flawed by conceit and rude behavior to possess security. Security is not necessarily found in how many years you have served or in how much you have invested. There are countless occasions where people have served for years, only to end up holding an empty bag. Do not get caught in the trap of thinking that your security is found in your leader, and the hand that they lend to help you. Your security has to solely be found in God, and not in any governing board, denominational discipline, or any man or woman. It is God who will plant you, and it is God who will keep you.

In other words, God's order will never be secondary to humankind's order. The point I am trying to convey is that when God establishes you and ordains you to a place, your security has to rest in the fact that it is God who ordered you to be there, not your leader. If by chance human will and human manipulation lead them to get rid of you or remove you from your leadership post, just remember God will provide and take care of you and the ministry that He has placed within you.

I once heard a notable preacher say, "It is my job to jump, and it is God's job to find me a place to land." This is the security you must have, therefore, so that your work may possess confidence, optimism, drive, and zeal. You can have these attributes when you learn where to put your trust. God has not called you to work in fear, looking over your shoulder to see whether or not you will be the order of the day at the meeting. You must do what God called you to do while trusting Him. Isaiah 54:4 reminds us, *Fear not; for thou shalt not be ashamed: neither be thou confounded; for thou shalt not be put to shame.*

LEADERSHIP RELATIONSHIP REFLECTION QUESTIONS

1. David had to learn how to serve under a leader that he knew was out to destroy him. Do you believe that David handled the situation correctly?

2. What is your idea of good leadership and bad leadership?

3. Has there ever been a misunderstanding between you and a leader you served under? If so, what did you do to correct the misunderstanding, and how did you maintain the relationship?

4. If a person tells you that they are involved in a bad leadership relationship, what advice would you offer them for making this bad relationship right?

5. How did David apply integrity, empathy, hope, and security in his relationship with Saul?

6. How did Saul violate integrity, empathy, hope, and security in his relationship with David?

CHAPTER 3

MAKING A WRONG
Business Relationship Right

*Then David got angry because of GOD's deadly outburst
against Uzzah. That place is still called Perez Uzzah
(The-Explosion-Against-Uzzah). David became fearful of
GOD that day and said, "This Chest is too hot to handle.
How can I ever get it back to the City of David?" He
refused to take the Chest of GOD a step farther. Instead,
David removed it off the road and to the house of Obed-
Edom the Gittite. The Chest of GOD stayed at the house of
Obed-Edom the Gittite for three months. And GOD pros-
pered Obed-Edom and his entire household.*

2 Samuel 6:8-11 MSG

Before we begin to discuss King David's business relationship specifically, let us focus first on God's perspective of
business, in general. One of the most effective ways to give
glory to God is through the establishment of a Christian
business. When the term "Christian business" is mentioned,

it is to suggest that while there is the operation of a legal entity such as a corporation, partnership, or proprietorship, the legal entity should reflect Christian values. If a Christian is truly committed to Jesus Christ and serving His purposes, then the business will be run according to His principles and precepts. Obviously, that means that a Christian must first understand God's rules.[1] The same standards should apply when we talk about being in partnership with someone in business.

According to Larry Burkett in his book, *The Complete Guide To Managing Money*, there are at least five functions of a Christian business: Evangelism, Discipleship, Financing God's Work, Providing for Needs, and Generating Profits.

The Evangelism of a Business

People in business come in contact with so many people throughout the day, and if you are in business or even working on business this is a good time to minister hope to people who are stressed out, frustrated, anxious, or despondent about something in life. Christian business owners often hang signs, play music or present some signal in their business to let people know where their loyalty lies. Chick-fil-A sends their signal by closing their stores on Sundays. It is important that you conduct business in such a way that people know for Whom you are ultimately working. (Colossians 3:23.)

The Discipleship of a Business

If there are people working in the business that is under your leadership, this is a good time for you to disciple them by modeling in front of them how Christians handle business. What you confess must be consistent with what you do, and you should always be mindful that once your team knows that you are a Christian, they will hold you to what you confess. They will look for you to help disciple them.

> *What you confess must be consistent with what you do.*

Financing God's Work in the Business

The difference between a Christian business establishment and a secular business establishment is that the Christian business is a means to not only provide sustainable income for the owners, but to also generate profits and resources to be used for the Kingdom. It is a good Christian business owner who will tithe off of both their business and their personal income. Millard Fuller, the founder of Habitat for Humanity, is a prime example of this principle. He was a very successful businessman who used his skills and resources to create an organization based on the principles of Christ which has helped provide housing for so many in need.

Providing for Needs Through the Business

A business must provide for the needs of its employees, creditors, customers, and owners. This is done by paying salaries, paying for supplies and equipment in a timely fashion, and providing a quality product at a fair price.[2]

Generating Profit from the Business

Proverbs 13:4 reminds us that, *Indolence wants it all and gets nothing; the energetic have something to show for their lives* (MSG). Nothing should replace good hard labor and the reward for that labor, from a business perspective, should be profit. Of course turning a profit is not just going to happen; you have to market, offer good service, manage well, budget, and cut cost where necessary. But do not feel guilty when God prospers your business, and be willing to give Him the glory when He does.

Returning to the story of David, when David discovered that his friend Uzzah was dead, he became utterly angry with God. In his mind, it did not make sense that God would take the life of a man who was protecting God's symbol of His presence. Keep in mind, however, that God did not kill Uzzah because He had nothing better to do or because He had a grudge against Uzzah. No, a divine precept had been established that the Ark of the Covenant was to be treated with great care and reverence for its holiness. Hence, it would have been better for the Ark of the Covenant to touch the ground that God made, than for a man of sinful nature to touch it.

Uzzah touched the Ark when the animal pulling the cart on which the Ark was being carried stumbled, causing the cart to jerk and the Ark to nearly fall from the cart. What was the Ark doing on a cart anyway? God instructed the Levites to carry the Ark on their shoulders, not put it on a cart. Because God's precept had been violated, Uzzah died, and David, like a child, began to pout and decided to set up a business deal with Obed-Edom to leave the Ark of the Covenant at his house.

The entire time the Ark of the Covenant was out of David's presence, David was depressed. His life did not reflect any passion, joy, vitality or zeal. Yet, the house of Obed–Edom had passion, joy, vitality, and zeal, simply because of their gratefulness to have the Ark of the Covenant, or God's presence, in their possession. It is when David sees how much joy Obed-Edom is receiving from this privilege that has been extended to him, that he decides to go and get the Ark of the Covenant back. When he has the Ark back in his possession, David again finds himself in a place of peace and restoration.

This account prompts some critical analysis about partnerships and business relationships. If ever there is a relationship that has the potential of going sour, it is a business relationship that does not have clear definition, boundaries, or guidelines. In every business relationship there are challenges and hard questions that we face. For instance, what is your motivation for establishing a business relationship? How do you handle it when you know you have made a bad business decision, and what relationship matters most at that point?

How do you cope when somebody else's business has favor, and yours is suffering financially? (Obed-Edom was prospering, and spiritually David was in a deficit.) How do you deal with the prosperity of another business, while you can't even get up enough money to make a start? Is it possible to establish an agreement with a friend contractually, without them feeling like you don't trust their friendship? Let us consider how to prevent some practices that lead to bad business relationships, while also learning from the life of David how to make a business relationship that has gone bad, right again.

The Motivation of a Business Relationship

David established a business deal with Obed-Edom for one reason—so Obed-Edom would house the Ark of the Covenant. This deal was struck with a very clear intention and motivation. If there is going to be an effective business relationship of any kind, it is important for you to know what you desire out of the relationship. Your motive in a matter has everything to do with the matter.

Your motive in a matter has everything to do with the matter.

Some time ago, I was invited to do training for the Tyson Food Corporation on "Diversity and Spirituality in the Workplace." I accepted this challenge because I admire the fact that the Tyson Company has chaplains in their facilities who are there to provide spiritual direction for people who are in need of spiritual, mental and emotional support. It is the philosophy of Tyson Foods that employees work better when they feel better.

In their request for my services, Tyson made it clear to me that in my presentation I needed to be comprehensive and pluralistic in my lecture. What this means is that while Tyson has strong Christian values, they also have people working in their facilities who represent other faiths and beliefs. While I am a Christian, in this business relationship I had to respect this reality of their company.

In my presentation, I talked about the principles of Christ as a standard, and presented His moral teachings with the hope that some of those in attendance would come to understand that Jesus Christ really is the Savior of the world. My business relationship experience with Tyson was a great one, because the terms of the business relationship were clearly defined and understood.

The Motivation of a Mission Statement

What is the mission of your business, and what is it that you are seeking to accomplish? A mission statement is very valuable in terms of establishing a relationship because it helps to fine tune the intention and the focus of the parties involved. It is imperative that everyone understands the common goal of the task. Once that common goal or mission is clear, all other plans, directives, and formulations will center around that.

A mission statement is very helpful in establishing a business relationship because when things begin to blossom and grow, when conflicts surface and differences of opinion begin to take root, most of the time it is the mission statement that can provide some clarity. It may not completely fix the problem, but at least the mission statement can hilight where there is common ground and possibly lead the way to resolution of disagreements.

Jesus gave a clarion call to his disciples in Matthew 28:19 when He said, *Go ye therefore, and teach all nations, baptizing them in the name of the Father, and of the Son, and of the Holy Ghost.* The mission was clear: 1) Go teach to all nations 2) Baptize them, too 3) Do it in the name of the Father and of the Son, and of the Holy Ghost. With a clear definition like this, no disciples should have been asking, "What do we do?" None should have been asking, "Do we baptize first, or do we teach first?" That was all made clear. Christ made it perfectly clear that all of this was to be done in the name of the Father, Son, and Holy Ghost. This is an example of a clear mission statement, and if your business relationship is going to be successful, then a clear mission statement like this is certainly needed.

The Motivation of a Ministry Call

Whenever someone talks about the establishment of a business relationship, it is often divorced from a ministry call. This should not be. Starting a business or a business relationship should be a ministry for a Christian. Too many times, we have limited ministry to the preacher, preaching on Sundays in a pulpit. Rarely does an entrepreneur understand that their personal business can also be classified as their ministry. Now I am not suggesting that if you start a business selling men's and women's fragrance, that you have a right to call yourself Minister Fragrance Supplier. The title is not necessary, what is necessary is that you you understand that your business is a vehicle for you to serve.

Your business is a vehicle for you to serve.

Once you sense your call to ministry, then you begin to attract people to be in partnership with you in a business relationship who have some commonality with your call. While commonality of purpose may not always exist with those whom your business serves, it should be a standard for those you actually partner with in your business enterprise. There needs to be a common goal of operation and call for the business relationship to be effective.

We see this concept in practice in Luke 5:4-7. When Jesus finished teaching, He said to Simon, *"Push out into deep water and let your nets out for a catch." Simon said, "Master, we've been fishing hard all night and haven't caught even a minnow. But if you say so, I'll let out the nets." It was no sooner said than done—a huge haul of fish, straining the nets past capacity. They waved to their partners in the other boat to come help them. They filled both boats, nearly swamping them with the catch* (MSG).

While it is very common to interpret this passage by celebrating the miracle catch of fish provided for Peter at the commissioning of Jesus, what I find even more amazing is that when Peter was blessed with the fish, he had so much that he had to call for "partners" to come and help him. I believe truly that these "partners" Peter called to help him were partners who first knew about fish, who then witnessed and understood that a miracle just happened. These were also partners who could, no doubt, celebrate with Peter. This is the kind of commonality that you should be seeking when praying about a business partner to help fill your boat with the blessings that God will provide through your business venture. You need a business partner with the knowledge base to help you, who can discern when God is doing miracles (which means it would help if they knew God), and who also knows that miracles are not always in the big, but sometimes the miracle is the Lord just simply sending one customer at a time. You need someone laboring with you who doesn't mind getting dirty with you, and who doesn't mind getting the "fish smell" on their hands if necessary.

Be faithful to your call and your business will be a success. Be careful to engage in business relationships with those who share or understand your call. You will have challenges, but challenges can be conquered when you understand your call.

The Motivation of the Missing Element

Finding the missing element is the key to any successful business. What is it that makes your business unique? What is it that you want to provide that is not already provided in the market? What is the business ministry you can provide that the enemy has been blocking where you are?

I have always been convinced that your millions are tied up in your passion. When you are passionate about your call to ministry, it is your passion that will attract your customer base. I know you are saying, "Well if my business explodes on the market, I won't be able to be seen everywhere my business will be represented." You are right, but your passion will be reflected in the building, the grounds, customer service, quality of product, and the consistency of excellence. When your business call is your passion, there is no drudgery in your business ministry. You will be empowered, you will have energy, you will be able to work long hours and it won't even feel like it. When you are operating in your passion, this is what will attract people to what you do.

Now to be realistic, just because your business call is your passion doesn't mean you don't have to have a business plan, a well thought out execution of ideas, consideration for financial backing, and legal advice for sound business practice. These things are still necessary.

Find the missing element, find the market need and meet that need with excellence. On your way to meeting the market need, don't forget the importance of building sound business relationships. It is wise to remember that when you are in business,

When you are in business, everybody is your customer.

everybody is your customer. Building relationships means you speak to people, realize that everybody has importance, learn from the success of others, and don't harbor a jealous spirit. Now go make your business ministry happen!

7 Sins that Can Destroy a Good Business Relationship

When the Bible talks about sin, it is very clear to say that all have sinned and come short of the glory of God. (Romans 3:23.) Not only have we all sinned, but without the gift of God through Jesus Christ, we would not even have access to eternal life, because the wages earned for sin is death. (Romans 6:23.) While sins run the gamut from lusting in the flesh to murdering another person, the Roman Catholic Church found a way to address moral behaviors and sin by categorizing sin into seven categories called, "The Seven Deadly Sins." While these seven deadly sins are not pinpointed in a particular scripture, these sins are represented throughout the Bible, collectively. In the eyes of God there is no small sin or big sin. The Roman Catholic Church has simply listed these sins as broad, sweeping categories that cover most of the failure found in humanity.

Rick Ezell describes *sin* as "Subsequential Internal Non-morality."[3] Another way of describing sin is to say that it is a drive that continually causes bad decisions which are motivated by an inadequacy that stems from human frailty.

This concept of sin is portrayed in Fredrick Buechner's novel entitiled, *Godric*. Godric's name means "God's Wreck," and the story opens by showing Godric as a homeless peddler who is in search of wealth. Godric's life is confused and conflicted, described perfectly by the Apostle Paul in Romans, chapter 7 when he says that what he knows to be the right thing to do he does not do it, while what he knows to be the wrong thing to do, he finds himself enjoying doing it. Seeking to fix himself, Godric becomes a recluse, a hermit who decides to separate himself from the world.

One night, Guilt got in the bed with him, and Godric found himself unable to sleep and rest, so he began to pray this prayer, "Lord, God....how useless is my life. I let folks call me Holy Father though I know myself to be of all God's sinful children most foul. My Flesh is ever prey to lust, pride, and sloth, and I need some saint to save me my soul, and teach me how to serve thee right."[4] Godric discovered that the wealth he was searching for could not fix him. It was a deeper relationship with the Savior that he needed more than anything.

When our relationship with Jesus as our Savior is not solid, it makes us desire things that we really don't need. Sin is a contamination and a corruption of desires, that has a debilitating affect upon any relationships that we seek to form. This is what the Catholic Church sought to convey through their sin formula called "The Seven Deadly Sins," which includes the sins of Pride, Envy, Anger, Sloth, Greed, Lust, and Gluttony.

The Sin of Pride in Business

The sin of Pride is listed first because it is the foundation on which all of the other sins are established. The sin of pride involves indulging one's own desires without regard for others. Pride has a way of becoming contagious in any environment in which it exists. Pride will make one refuse to acknowledge problem areas, and will keep one living in denial about their reality. A person engaged in the sin of pride will only see what is good for themselves, and will do only what is right according to their own will. A person engaged in the sin of pride can continually practice this sin, while seeking to justify their actions to suit their own purposes. A person engaged in the sin of pride will see something good that is happening, but refuse to celebrate it because it does not celebrate them.

This sin of pride hinders any business relationship because it contradicts team building and teamwork. When a business relationship is polluted by pride, that relationship is naturally established upon denial and dishonesty. We must reject pride to see the truth in a situation. Sometimes the truth is that the numbers do not fall in the profit category, sometimes the truth is that the service was not up to par, sometimes the truth is that the business is struggling and changes need to happen. These things are difficult to acknowledge when pride pollutes your motivation in business. Therefore, if you are seeking to establish a solid business relationship, your first step should be to ask God to show you if the relationship is prayerful or prideful.

Embracing a sense of humility does not mean you must live in weak submission.

If the relationship is tainted by sinful pride, you must make this right. Making a prideful business relationship right starts by embracing a sense of humility. Embracing a sense of humility does not mean you must live in weak submission. Humility is about being able to hear the input of others, it is about developing tolerance to receive criticism and realizing that things can always be improved. If you are establishing a new business relationship, make sure you are connecting with someone who demonstrates humility, someone who understands that in order for the partnership to work, there must be an eradication of sinful pride.

The Sin of Envy In Business

The sin of Envy is manifested in a dread of the success of another. It is interesting to me that the people who really seem to be blessed by God are those who don't mind seeing others blessed by God. The word *envy* comes from the Latin word *invidia*, which means "to look viciously upon." Envy runs deep. It is the cousin to hate, malice, evil, and corruption. "Envy is directed toward people who are close to us....Two people of the same age and similar interest feel envy most keenly. Doctors envy doctors, lawyers envy lawyers, preachers envy preachers. Neighbor envies neighbor, manager envies manager, sales person envies sales person. One is more apt to envy another of equal standing and status."[5] If you seek to develop a business relationship with anyone, by all means get a partner who is secure within himself. This is important because success happens when you focus on what makes you unique, not when you focus on the success of another. If your business partner is not secure, it is just a matter of time before the competition of another business turns their head and your relationship becomes a competition between the two of you.

It is one thing to fight in the ring, it is another thing to fight in your own corner.

It is one thing to fight in the ring, it is another thing to fight in your own corner.

Guarding against the sin of envy means that you and your business partner must learn how to celebrate your strengths, what makes your business thrive, and what makes your business unique. Concentrate on those areas where God has blessed your business and on what you are praying for God to do in your business, and also pray that God will do His good work in somebody else's business, even if the business you are praying for is your competition.

The Sin of Anger in Business

The sin of Anger is a little different from the sin of Envy. The sin of Envy deals with emotion, while the sin of Anger deals with acting on that emotion. When I think of the sin of

Anger, I am reminded of one who steps on a nail. If you have ever stepped on a nail, you know that it is important to get the nail out as soon as possible. If the nail remains in the foot, the wound can become infected and cause other problems with the foot. Anger is the same way. If you do not take anger out of a relationship, it will surely spread and become a serious infection that will later on be difficult to treat.

The sin of Anger can become so vicious that it will cause people to rob, cheat, steal and even kill. Angry people act off of impulse, and then spend much time apologizing and feeling guilty. Angry people can destroy an atmosphere, and then transfer their anger on to people who are not even directly involved with the situation that prompted the anger in the first place.

If you are seeking to have a good business or a good business relationship, you must deal with those things that trigger your "anger button." If you are a person who loves to be on time, your anger button might be triggered when people show up late. When things are not placed in the order that you prefer, you may have to resist pushing your anger button and instead remind yourself that most of the time, things can be re-ordered to suit your purposes. If there is a certain personality type that just gets on your "reserve nerve"(that is the nerve after the last nerve), then you must learn to refrain from pushing that anger button. If you respond with something like, "That was stupid," "I hate you for doing this," "You make my life miserable," these types of anger words cannot be taken back and will ultimately hurt your business and your business relationship, sometimes in ways that you can never recover.

The Sin of Sloth in Business

The sin of Sloth in a business manifests itself with laziness, uncaring attitudes, non-nurturing actions, and a lack of a spirit of excellence. Sloth comes from the Latin word *acedia*, which means a lack of caring, or an indifference to responsibility to self, God, or others.

This particular sin in a business can be detrimental because if you don't work the business, the business won't work. Sloth is a dangerous sin because it refuses to do what is necessary for success, it puts the responsibility on someone else, and it does not discern a sense of urgency, thereby denying an opportunity to make a difference in vital areas. When there is a spirit of sloth, relationship building is very difficult because the slothful person refuses to put forth the energy, time and sacrifice that it takes to build the relationship. In other words, a slothful person in a business couldn't care less about making sure that their clients are satisfied with their service. They refuse to discipline co-workers for providing less than excellent service and they will continue to make up excuses as to why a task was not completed. Slothful people may even go so far as to blame others for their failures.

For people in business who are slothful, it is not that they don't have ability, but they just believe in using their most powerful weapon—procrastination. Procrastination leads to jobs that are incomplete, not well thought out, and done as more of a response than a reason. "This sin believes in nothing, cares for nothing, seeks to know nothing, interferes with nothing, enjoys nothing, loves nothing, hates nothing, finds purpose in nothing, and lives for nothing, and remains alive only because it would die from nothing."[6]

An indifferent attitude and a slothful spirit hurt any relationship because relationships require work, effort, understanding, and initiative. A slothful person gives no thought to sacrifice, and contributing to the success of the enterprise is not even considered. Consider the time the chicken and the pig were having a conversation.

Relationships require work, effort, understanding, and initiative.

The discussion centered around which one meant more to a breakfast. The chicken said, "I do, because I contribute eggs. What is a breakfast without eggs?" The pig said, "Well that's just a contribution, but I make a sacrifice. I have to die before I'm served at breakfast." The chicken made a contribution, the pig made a sacrifice. A person with a slothful spirit does not see the importance of either sacrificing or contributing. They are slow to contribute if they do at all, and like to merely talk about sacrifice as actual sacrifice is highly unlikely from a slothful person.

Beware of developing business relationships with slothful people. God has destined your business to prosper and be blessed, and it is important that you partner with people who connect with you in your effort to create a business of excellence. Interestingly, slothful people rarely make room in their lives for anybody else—there is a time when you should be thankful for that fact.

The Sin of Greed in Business

It was some time ago when Ivan Boesky was the shining star of Wall Street, but later went to prison and paid a healthy fine of $100 million dollars for his crimes. Prior to his conviction for crimes involving insider trading, Boesky spoke at the University of California at Berkely. In his speech he said, "Greed is alright, by the way I want you to know that. I think greed is healthy. You can be greedy, and still feel good about yourself."[7] Greed is an insatiable desire to have and possess more, it is a drive and a thirst for obtaining more of something that one already possesses.

Greed is an insatiable desire to have and possess more.

Most of the time when empires, civilizations, nations, and institutions fall, they usually fall because of this sin called greed. This sin in a business paradigm is usually detrimental because it affects the integrity of the business. For example, if there is a restaurant in business who charges 18% gratuity to a party of three, when the menu clearly says that this amount should only be applied to parties of 6 or more people, it is clear that this restaurant is willing to risk their integrity for greed. When greed gets into a person's spirit, it has a way of distracting from good judgment, sound decision making, and reasonable actions. One of the worst reputations that a business person can have is to be considered one who will do anything for a dollar.

Beware involving yourself in a business relationship with a person who is possessed by greed. If you find yourself in such a situation, you must have a good system of checks and balances in place because when a person is greedy, sometimes they will even steal from themselves if in the end it means they will obtain more. In a business relationship with a greedy person, discernment and awareness are key, and non-negotiable.

In your business interactions, you may face the temptation to get more, but having more does not always mean you are more blessed. You are blessed when you have peace. You are blessed when you can go home and go to sleep at night because of a clear conscience. You are blessed when you know from Whom your provisions come, and it must be clear that there is no need to be greedy, because it is the Lord who will provide.

When establishing a business relationship, one must consider sufficiency. Sufficiency is determined by necessity, and necessity is often shaped by desire. Controlled desires will inevitably result in honest deeds. Make sure quality is the goal when seeking out business relationships, not how much more can be obtained. Your relationships should be about building the greatness of your business and not about the greed of a business.

The Sin of Lust in Business

Lusting is the sin of having an intense desire for flesh, money, or material. Lusting is passion for these things that has grown out of control. First John 2:16 says, *For all that is in the world, the lust of the flesh, and the lust of the eyes, and the pride of life, is not of the Father, but is of the world.* Lusting is a force that pulls one to engage in something that has the potential to overtake their self-discipline and control.

It is interesting to me that when advertisers seek to sell a product, the first intentional move is to appeal to eyes, ears, smell, and our need to touch. For an example, the other week I received a call from our local BMW car dealership inviting me to come drive one of their brand new BMWs. While initially I felt honored that they would think about me in this regard, it occurred to me that a financial trap for me was lying ahead. What the sales person knew was that if he could just get me in the car and let my nose smell that new car smell, let my eyes see all of the new amenities, let me hear him talk about all of the reasons I should invest in this car, he knew that if he could appeal to my senses, my senses could talk me into buying that car. Lust works in the same fashion, once lust is captured by your senses, shortly after you may find yourself engaging in activity that can be destructive to you and your business.

If any business relationship is going to be successful then it is important for those who are in partnership to pray for strength against the spirit of lust. This is particularly important if there is a business relationship between a professional man and a professional woman. Think about it, if the enemy wants to destroy a business effort between a man and a woman, it would naturally be part of his tactic to entice them to come together before he tears them apart. How common is the story of a man and a woman who start out strictly as professionals, performing a task and doing a job. After both spend hours away from their families, over into the late evening, tired and wearied from the day, they end up at dinner together. In this relaxed environment, they engage in conversation about personal problems and feelings. After a few drinks, the conversation has now moved from business to inadequacies with their marriage, children, and even their broken dreams. A vulnerable mood is at the table, and a longing to be touched sets in. Thoughts of work are abandoned and moral failures occur. This is a business relationship where lust took over the mission and the purpose for which the two initially came together.

There is a danger in allowing lust to enter a business relationship. As soon as the hint is given and the emotions are aroused, the business relationship changes. The consequences of unchecked lust can be detrimental and far reaching. Business decisions are now driven by emotions and not sound judgment. Personal issues are

The consequences of unchecked lust can be detrimental and far reaching.

now interwoven with professional issues. Conflict is sure to arise in the relationship, which could compromise the mission of the business. If the relationship ends, most of the time the business does, too. The threat of sexual harassment can be used to soothe hurt emotions. In the end, managing the business is always easier than managing emotions.

While some personal relationships evolve from business relationships and are very successful, most of the time these kinds of situations simply involve other factors that prove too stressful on the business relationship. Is all of this in the name of lust worth the millions that you can earn together, the lives that you can impact together, the reputation that you developed thus far? Are you willing to see it all destroyed because of one night of pleasure? Is this worth your family, children, your spouse or career? Is it worth disappointing the God who gave you the business vision and plan in the first place?

Making a business relationship that has been damaged by lust, right, starts with putting your mind back on the things of God and the destiny that God has purposed for you.

The Sin of Gluttony in Business

The sin of Gluttony is best described as the sin of one indulging excessively in eating or drinking. While this sin may not naturally be applied to business, Rick Ezell in his book, *The 7 Sins of Highly Defective People*, takes a deeper look at the issue of gluttony and what can particularly drive one to this behavior. Ezell suggest that gluttony is really about gaining power, control, and becoming a master of devouring.

GAINING POWER

It is interesting to me that gluttony is relative to power. The idea here is that gluttony is about the exertion of power that enables one to eat whatever they desire. The power to choose the when, the what, and the where gives a sense of significance to the one who is indulging. In other words, if a person does not feel like they have any power in their home environment, on their job, in the church or even in their social circles, the one place where they can exercise power is in their eating. They may not be able to control others, but they do have the power to control those cheese covered fries, triple decked burger, and that oversized chocolate cake for dessert. The gluttonous person feels a sense of empowerment, when in fact gluttonous behaviors really reflect the lack of will power to say no to some food that we know will eventually become detrimental to our health.

In a business relationship, a person may demonstrate these power issues particularly when they don't have power anywhere else. If this is the case, then in the business operation you may see signs of exertion of severe authority when it is not necessary. You may see hints of insecurity when their territory is threatened, you may even sense a need for them to acquire more of a thing because it makes them feel powerful and in control.

To make this wrong relationship right, it is important that you realize that you can't change people, but you also can't give in to their need to feel empowered if giving in would be detrimental to the business. There may be instances, however, where you can give them a title and responsibility where they can exercise an appropriate measure of power. Just beware if you choose this route, that the person's perception not become skewed so that they begin to desire inappropriate measures of power after getting that initial taste.

CONTROL

When I was young, one of the things that I really enjoyed doing was riding the most thrilling roller coaster that I could find. I would even ride it several times. I loved the thrill I would feel all the way down in my stomach, and the nervous feeling that the steep drop on the coaster would give. However, I noticed that the older I became, the less I enjoyed the roller coaster. I realized that the roller coaster would cause me to feel like I wasn't in control. That feeling in my stomach was no longer fun. I found myself anxiously anticipating what the next drop was going to be like, rather than relaxing and just enjoying the risky thrill.

As I continue to get older, it seems I grow more determined to control certain facets of my life. Certain things like the roller coaster remind me that really, I am not in control. When I was young, control didn't matter, but as I get older it becomes more significant and important.

There are many people who feel their life is like a roller coaster. They find themselves being nervous about the next turn, anxious about the upcoming drop and the turn that would snap their body a certain way. In short, they feel out of control over their future, not certain of what is going on with their family, not to mention their finances and their job security in a failing economy. The only thing they find comfort in controlling is the food they choose to consume in a gluttonous fashion.

This need for gluttonous control can show up in a business relationship. Because a person is nervous about the future, frantic about the next turn in the economy, and functioning as a pessimist, they find themselves controlling things in the business relationship that they really don't need to control. While every business venture is a risk, business ventures must also involve faith. There are some things in a business that can be controlled such as procedures, guidelines, inventory, and business image. However, there are other areas that you can't control. You can't control the stock market and the level of people's spending comfort. You can't control whether a customer is picky, when nothing that you do will please them. You can't control the level of excellence that your competition may offer. The only thing you can control is you.

When you find yourself in a bad business relationship in this regard, the way to make it right is to help the people you partner with in business understand that the fate of the business is in God's hand, and that fact means that you are not in this by yourselves. Successfully dealing with control issues also involves knowing how to find good in the company of trial. A good public relations person will tell you that that there is good PR in every moment of exposure. It is what you do with the exposure that makes the difference.

Recently, I had a friend who purchased a new Toyota vehicle. Initially I asked why she did this, considering all of the problems that have been reported about Toyota vehicles. She said that the car salesman made a statement to her that made her feel comfortable. The salesman said, "Ma'am since we have had some challenges, we are checking and double checking every vehicle that leaves this lot to make certain that it is safe. All of your features have been checked, and this car is probably safer than any other car you can purchase from any other car lot. If ever there was a good time to buy a Toyota, now is the time, because all of these problems have made them scrutinize every car more cautiously since they now know that they are under the gun." Sometimes, it's not what happens to you, it is how you flip it. Release control and embrace God.

Sometimes, it's not what happens to you, it is how you flip it.

Master of Devouring

When you consider the Native American approach to killing a wolf, it is quite interesting. The Native Americans had what they called knife traps. The hunter would take a knife and stick the handle into the ground, with the blade protruding out of the ground. The hunter would then blanket the blade with blood from venison, and let the blood freeze on the blade. This scheme was done knowing that when the wolf would approach the knife, the wolf would begin licking the frozen blood off of the knife. As the heat from the wolf's mouth melted the blood that he was licking off of the knife, eventually one of the licks would cut his tongue right down the middle. While the wolf was devouring the blood off of the knife, he ended up licking a blade.

Unfortunately some people treat food the same way, not knowing that what they are devouring without any restraint can eventually lead to their death. Devouring is more of a discipline issue, it is one thing to eat, but it is another to devour. Devouring speaks to being relentless, not caring about outcome, being aggressive for self-satisfaction.

This master of devouring practice can show up in a business relationship. When there is a devouring spirit on your team, this person is liable to do anything to anybody, as long as they are getting what they want. This wolf-like mentality may intimidate others, but it doesn't matter to the devouring partner because they just simply want what they want. They attack like there is no tomorrow, as if the only thing that matters is the deal that it is on the table now.

If you are currently in business with a person like this, or if you are even considering it, know that much of your time is going to be spent recovering from their mistakes, apologizing for their actions, and spending money to do things over, because devouring does not reflect wisdom. Yes, there is a certain aggressiveness that you do want in your business, but as a Christian, your business must reflect a right temperament as well.

Action Steps to Make a Wrong Business Relationship Right

1. If you are in business with a person who has a different perspective about how the business should function, it important that time be given to revisit the vision, make sure that expectations are aligned, and more importantly, confirm that this is still a good fit for you and your business.

2. If you are in business with a person who continually causes confusion, disrespects you and others, or does not have the right temperament, it is important that you treat this situation by applying wisdom. When there is a person involved with your business like this, count the cost. What is this person costing you? What relationships is the person hurting? Can your reputation or finances afford those hurts? If you find that the relationship is doing more harm than good, start now to put a plan together to sever the ties.

3. If you are in a business relationship where harassment is an issue, note that this is a very serious offense. If you are being harassed because of your sex, religion, or race, know that the law is on your side. You don't have to tolerate

mistreatment, but it is a smart thing to make certain that what you are feeling is factual and not a result of any insecurity on your part. Keep detailed documents, text messages, and e-mails. If you ever have to prove your case, these pieces of material will be very helpful.

4. If you are in a business relationship where your emotions have taken over, to make this situation right is going to involve a degree of separation, whether it is physical, emotional or spiritual. Breaking emotional soul ties are difficult, however this can happen when you put your trust back in God, strengthen your esteem, circle yourself with other positive environments, and rebuke the spirit of the people who disappointed or violated you.

BUSINESS RELATIONSHIP
REFLECTION QUESTIONS

1. Explain why a good relationship between business partners is vital to the success of any business.

2. If you were to start a business or if you currently have a business, what is the motivation, mission, and the missing element of your business?

3. Have you ever been in a wrong business relationship? What happened and what role did you play in the incident? How did you manage the conflict? What did you do, if anything, to make it right?

4. Of the 7 deadly sins, which sin seems to be your greatest temptation? How does that sin hinder you from developing solid relationships?

5. What business relationships are you willing to make right as a result of reading this book?

CHAPTER 4

MAKING A WRONG
Soul Mating Relationship Right

"Come outside," said Jonathan. "Let's go to the field."
When the two of them were out in the field, Jonathan said,
"As GOD, the God of Israel, is my witness, by this time
tomorrow I'll get it out of my father how he feels about
you. Then I'll let you know what I learn. May GOD do his
worst to me if I let you down! If my father still intends to
kill you, I'll tell you and get you out of here in one piece.
And GOD be with you as he's been with my father! If I
make it through this alive, continue to be my covenant
friend. And if I die, keep the covenant friendship with my
family—forever. And when GOD finally rids the earth of
David's enemies, stay loyal to Jonathan!" Jonathan
repeated his pledge of love and friendship for David. He
loved David more than his own soul!

I Samuel 20:11-17 MSG

David partnered with Obed-Edom to accomplish a task,
but his soul mate was Jonathan—the son of his enemy, Saul.

Because of Jonathan and David's documented close relation-ship, some have unjustly accused Jonathan and David of having a sensual love affair with one another. This chapter will address ways to overcome speculations and criticisms of mis-diagnosed relationships. This chapter will also give a picture of what a real soul mating relationship looks like, along with practical tips to recognize your soul mate, and suggestions on how to strengthen relationships with the same gender without those relationships lending to any impure practices. There are times when men must keep it real with men, and women need relationships where they can keep it real with other women. This chapter will give insight on how to develop these kinds of relationships.

It is most interesting to note that at the same time David was Saul's chief enemy, he was also the best friend of his son, Jonathan. Not only were they friends, but Jonathan and David are referred to as being knitted at the soul. There have been some who have tried to pervert this scripture, in an attempt to link Jonathan and David in a homosexual relationship. This assertion is not at all supported by the scriptures, but it reveals the need for dialogue about how we can create an atmosphere for men to be good friends with men, and women to be good friends with women without their relationship prompting even the mere suggestion of homosexual activity. I firmly believe that people can have a friendship so close that they connect at the soul with others, without there ever being any practice of homosexuality or lesbianism which, according to scripture, is an abomination before God. (Leviticus 20:13.)

The term "soul mate" is actually a term that has its origins in Greek culture. It is used commonly to describe a very close, trusted, reliable, and spiritual relationship. A *soul mate* is somebody with whom one has a feeling of deep and natural affinity, love, and compatibility that is often referred to as a twin flame or twin soul.

The idea of soul mates was initially introduced to us in Greek mythology by Aristophanes in his speech from Plato's Symposium.[1] The myth was that humans existed once with four arms, four legs, and one head with two faces. When humankind was in this state, each human was unusually strong, fast on their feet, and had tremendous mobile ability. The myth holds that it was Zeus who unveiled the plan to break down and humble the human creature because he feared their strength, so Zeus devised a plan to split man in half, subjecting him for the rest of his life to searching for his other half to complete him. According to this myth, this is the reason that we only have two arms, two legs, and two feet.

Putting Greek mythology aside, as Christians we are clearly convinced that we are beautifully and wonderfully made in the image of God. God created us from the source of His own elements—the dust of the earth. However, even Christians often use the term "soul mate" and spend a considerable amount of time searching and looking for the "one" that God has knitted us with at the soul. Though Christianity

God has designed us to live in community with others.

does not purport the mythological story of soul mating, God has designed us to live in community with others. When we use phrases like "prayer partner," "our spirits connect," or even "my inner circle," whether it is conscious or unconscious, we are making reference to connecting with people who in some way connect with our soul. "A soul mate is someone to whom we feel profoundly connected, as though the communication and communing that take place between us were not the product of intentional efforts, but rather a divine grace. This kind of relationship is so important to the soul that many have said there is nothing more precious in life."[2]

Jesus had his "inner circle," "prayer partners," and "spirit connectors" who one could easily call His "soul mates." Even though Jesus had twelve disciples with Him, there were three—Peter, James, and John—who He more passionately connected with. It was this "inner circle" that Jesus relied upon, and even depended on to watch Him while He tarried in prayer in Gethsemane. This "inner circle" undoubtly saw and heard some things that the other nine didn't. It was while they were with Him in the Garden, that Jesus began to pray until great drops of blood fell from His face. But after Jesus had spent His initial time in prayer and went back to check on the three "inner circle" disciples, He found they had fallen asleep. Jesus then said to these, *"Could you not watch with Me one hour?"* (Matthew 24:36-40 NKJV.)

It is by studying the experience that Jesus had with those close to Him, that we can develop a paradigm for discovering our soul mates and even determining how we must choose people who we will allow to be connected to us closely.

How to Identify a Soul Mate

SOUL MATES MAKE THEMSELVES AVAILABLE

I contend that the reason Jesus asked Peter, James, and John to go with Him was because perhaps He didn't feel that they would hesitate about heeding His request. You will be able to identify your soul mate because there will be an ease in knowing that whatever you ask, they will do it to the best of their ability. I have many friends, but if I ever go through a storm, there are only a hand full of people that my spirit feels comfortable enough with to call and ask to come and stand with me. The reason for this ease in making requests of them, seems to stem from the fact that, many times when your soul is in a particular place, your soul mate will understand without you even having to say a word.

I was attending a workshop on relationships some time ago, and the facilitator said something that struck me. He said that one of the greatest experiences you can have with someone is to just *be with* someone. Being with them does not require much stress or strain, you are able to just be there. It's just an easy feeling that you have, you feel secure being together.

SOUL MATES WILL CONNECT WITH YOU ON SPIRITUAL MATTERS

It would almost be an oxymoron for someone to say the words "soul mate" and not talk about that term's relationship to spirituality. People interpret scriptures, sermons, teachings, readings, and events in many different ways. However, when you connect with a soul mate, often times you will be able to share similarity in interpretation of certain events and experiences.

When I was a young pastor in my first church, the Lord linked me with a very special chairman of my Deacons ministry who became somewhat of a father figure to me. While we both were clear that I was the pastor, this man would offer me fatherly advice on matters of the church and life in general. I will never forget that one Easter Sunday when, while preaching, I completely lost my voice. Later on I would discover that I had a severe case of acid reflux, but at this time, the reason for my loss of voice escaped me. When I lost my voice while preaching, I took my seat for moment and had the choir sing another selection while I sipped on some hot tea. After that song selection, my chairman stood up to the microphone and said to the congregation, "The pastor's voice is gone, but God is leading me to finish his message."

At that point, this man stood up and proceeded to preach my message. I need to add that on that Sunday, he did it better than I would have done it. In his message he talked about some things that I was going to talk about, though we had never had a discussion about my message. How could this be? I had a chairman of the Deacons ministry who was able to connect with my soul for the ministry, and thank God I did. Soul mating is about connecting spiritually, and being there with a voice, when the other doesn't have one.

> *Soul mating is about connecting spiritually.*

SOUL MATES DO NOT REGARD TIME

When Jesus asked the disciples to go and pray with Him, it was late in the evening. So late, in fact, that they could not stay awake to pray. We have criticized the disciples for not staying awake, but what I would like to celebrate with them is that they never told Jesus it was too late for them to go in the first place.

Often times when your soul is agonizing over something, time is not a factor you consider. If a person is connected to your soul, even though they need sleep, they can feel when you are agonizing. Soul mates have a way of making you feel like you can access them at any time, and that whatever your need, whenever you need it, it is not a problem. I don't want to make a soul mating relationship sound like utopia or the epitome of a perfect relationship, but I will say that most of the time, two souls who are knitted together know how to recognize when sacrifice is needed.

Even though these disciples went to sleep, what we can't argue with is that they never complained about "having to go" with Jesus. They went in spite of the lateness of the hour. Henry Van Dyke once said, "Time is too slow for those who wait, too swift for those who fear, too long for those who grieve, too short for those who rejoice, but for those who love, time is eternity."

Soul Mates Are Not Perfect, They Do Make Mistakes

If you are not careful, you can miss your soul mate by looking for someone who is perfect. Most of the time, even if a person is your soul mate, they are still prone to have imperfections that may literally get on your nerves. Watch this, most of the time they may get on your nerves, because *you* get on your nerves. If they are in some way a twin to your soul, the things that bother you about you, will be magnified when they do to you what you do to yourself. I know that sounds like a tongue twister, but it is true.

When Jesus asked the disciples, *"Could you not watch with Me one hour,"* essentially there was a part in His question that reminded Him of Himself. It was Jesus who had just asked His Father, *"Let this cup pass from me"* (Matthew 26:39). He was fighting with temptation, and the disciples were, too. He saw a part of Himself, in them.

Your soul mate may be full of imperfections, but it's not what they do right or wrong that will connect you. It is your commonality of purpose that will connect you, and when there is a common purpose, then most of the time you can find a way to deal with the imperfections.

Soul Mates Will Make It Easy for You to Forgive

While Jesus prayed, the disciples fell asleep. When Jesus discovered that those to whom his soul was connected had fallen asleep, notice that Jesus did not get angry with them or even dismiss them. He simply returned back to His assignment, while they remained in a slumber. Maybe the reason it was so easy for Jesus to forgive the error of the disciples was because Jesus Himself was dealing with the reality of His own temptation. While His temptation was to avoid the cross, their temptation was to sleep. We know that the disciples lost their battle with temptation and slept rather than prayed, as Jesus had asked them to do. Thank God, Jesus overcame His temptation and because of His great love, He suffered death on the cross.

When soul mates connect, very seldom do they part over petty issues

When Jesus finds the disciples asleep, He does not get angry with them, He simply returns back to His assignment. When you really connect with your soul mate, there are some things that you won't allow to come between the two of you. When soul mates connect, very seldom do they part over petty issues like who's going to pay for lunch this time, what you said hurt my feelings, or wondering who is going to make it to the top first. Soul mates do not allow issues to come between them. They recognize them, deal with them, maybe even fuss over them, and then move on. Soul mates do a great job of prioritizing what is important and what is not for their relationship. Most often, the common denominator between both of them is the gift to be able to forgive the other for the good of the relationship and for the benefit of what they both are called to accomplish.

Soul Mates Are Not Limited to One Person in Their Life

Isn't it interesting that Jesus didn't ask all twelve disciples to go with Him to the Garden, nor did He just ask one to go. He requested three of them to go. This would indicate that He considered more than one disciple to be in His inner circle, to be one of His soul mates. This would confirm that it is possible for you to have more than one soul mate, as well. It is at this point that we diverge from the traditional teaching of Greek mythology concerning soul mates, because the Greeks believed that there is only one person—one half of your soul—for which you are searching. But because we believe that God is able to duplicate His Spirit in thousands at one time, it is possible for a person to have more than one soul mate. Why? Because to say that God only has one soul mate for your life is like saying that God only has one prophet to preach His Word, or one disciple to do His will. God knows how to send the right people into your life so that when the season of one person is up, God has a way of introducing someone else for the next season.

CHARACTERISTICS OF PEOPLE THAT MAY NOT FIT YOUR SOUL

It is important that those in your most intimate, innermost circle of friends possess characteristics that fit your soul. Avoid people who are abrasive, abusive, argumentative, closed-minded, critical, defiant, in denial, dishonest, domineering, evasive, impatient, indecisive, insecure, intolerant, irritable, irresponsible, jealous, overly sensitive, pessimistic, repressed, resentful, secretive, self-deceptive, selfish, self-centered, shallow, stubborn, tactless, vain, quick tempered, and/or withdrawn.

Christians must see soul mates differently than what Greek mythology purports. They must view soul mates from God's perspective. Edgar Cayce, the famous "sleeping prophet," defined twin souls or soul mates as souls who come together to achieve a joint task. The soul mate in your life must meet this definition. Who is it in your life that you trust enough to help you complete a task? Who is it in your life that you can be totally yourself around, and not be concerned about consequences if you make a mistake? Who knows the pulse of your heartbeat, and what you are most passionate about? Who is it that you know is praying for you, even when you are not praying for yourself? Whoever it is that comes to your mind when you think of these questions, more than likely not, that is a person assigned by God to be your soul mate. Learn to enjoy this relationship, and take it for the gift that it is.

A soul mate relationship does not automatically imply sexual intimacy. To say that it does, incorrectly limits the definition of soul mate. The soul mating relationship is much broader than that. If the Spirit of God has joined two people, then two males can be spiritual soul mates without any hint of sexual overtones. They are just innocent boys, by the nod of one head, the other knows exactly what he is communicating. It's a syncopation and oneness that is shared between the two. Nothing intimate, just full of spirit.

It is the same for two women. It is possible to be spiritual soul mates without perverse overtones. Women are naturally more drawn to bonding, anyway. Women generally are nurturers, emotional beings, and many of them like to make physical contact while they are communicating. They even refer to each other as "girlfriends" which is a generic term of endearment between women. (You never hear men calling one another "boyfriends"—nor should you!) So when you see two women interacting in this way, please do not minimize their bonding moment to lesbianism. The depth of commitment between soul mates goes far beyond sexual encounters. We must recognize proper soul mating relationships and celebrate when others finally come across their sincere, Spirit-filled, soul mate.

How to Make a Wrong Soul Mating Relationship Right

The way you make a soul mating relationship right is by reshaping and expanding one's mindset about what God intends a soul mate to be. Don't limit your definition of soul mate to just erotic lovers. This gift of God is much more far reaching than that. Soul mating is a spiritual matter in which people bond at a deeper level, and it is possible for soul mates to come in any gender.

SOUL MATE RELATIONSHIP REFLECTION QUESTIONS

1. After reading this chapter, do you think that the term "soul mate" should be applied to Christians who are seeking solid relationships with other Christians?

2. How do you define a soul mate? Have you ever had one?

3. Soul mate relationships have typically been viewed as romantic or erotic unions. Do you think it is possible for two people of the same gender to be soul mates without being a lesbian or a homosexual?

4. In the section "How to Identify a Soul Mate," which characteristic would you say you strongly exhibit in your relationships?

5. Have you ever thought that a person was your soul mate, and then later you discovered that they were not? How did you handle this discovery, and what things did you seek to do to make the relationship right?

6. What are some things that you need to do for yourself to make you a better friend or soul mate?

CHAPTER 5

MAKING A WRONG
Love Relationship Right

David, ceremonially dressed in priest's linen, danced with great abandon before GOD. The whole country was with him as he accompanied the Chest of GOD with shouts and trumpet blasts. But as the Chest of GOD came into the City of David, Michal, Saul's daughter, happened to be looking out a window. When she saw King David leaping and dancing before GOD, her heart filled with scorn.

David returned home to bless his family. Michal, Saul's daughter, came out to greet him: "How wonderfully the king has distinguished himself today—exposing himself to the eyes of the servants' maids like some burlesque street dancer!" David replied to Michal, "In GOD's presence I'll dance all I want! He chose me over your father and the rest of our family and made me prince over GOD's people, over Israel. Oh yes, I'll dance to GOD's glory—more recklessly even than this. And as far as I'm concerned ... I'll gladly look like a fool ... but among these maids you're so worried about, I'll be honored no end."

Michal, Saul's daughter, was barren the rest of her life.

2 Samuel 6:14-16, 20-23 MSG

When David was dancing before the Lord, his wife got jealous, accused him of exposing himself before women, and told him he was too sophisticated to be dancing like that. David makes this wrong relationship right, not by becoming overly critical, but by remaining firm in his position. He does not compromise his relationship with or passion for God, but he seeks to introduce his wife to the Lord by just merely talking about the Lord and His faithfulness. This chapter will discuss ways to strengthen a love relationship when it has been thrown off balance by envy or because one does not understand the commitment that the other has to God. This chapter will also offer some marriage strategies and activities that can help strengthen the marital relationship.

One of the greatest movies I have seen in a long time, is the movie *Avatar.* I enjoyed this movie so much that I saw it three times! After seeing this movie, I can understand why it holds the distinction as the best selling movie of all time. On the screen, you are captivated with gripping cinematography, with the fluorescent colors that draw you into the emotions and passions of planet Pandora, not to mention the three dimensional graphics which allow you to see this epic movie from a panoramic view. But in the midst of all of these gripping images, what made the movie really captivating for me was the significance that it places on the value of relationships.

In this movie you are drawn into the relationship between the Sky People and their military prowess, and the relationship between the Na'Vi people and the sacred tree. However, the most significant relationship in the movie is the relationship between Jake and Neytiri. There were times in the movie when Jake and Neytiri would communicate with one another by saying simply, "I see you," meaning I see how you are feeling, because of my relationship with you, I already know where your soul is located.

There was a subtle, yet intimate moment between these two characters in the movie, when they connected their hair. Throughout the movie it seemed that both Jake and Neytiri would resolve differences and get in tune with one another as if their agendas were synchronized. When I saw this scene when the hair of these two characters was connected, it occurred to me how beautiful it would be if relationships were that simple—if we could just connect hair to hair, and then naturally all problems, all conflict, all relationship challenges would resolve. While this may happen on planet Pandora, this is not at all the reality for most love relationships. I am afraid to say, it takes a little more than just connecting hair.

How do you deal with your love relationship when the connection is broken? How do you confront the challenges in your relationship when there is no compatibility in the spirit and confusion is dominating the conversation? How do you make this wrong love relationship right?

In 2 Samuel 6, David is now returning back home with the Ark of the Covenant. He is so ecstatic about having the Ark back, he can't help but dance with all his might before the

Lord. It is while David is dancing, that his excitement causes him to dance out of his ephod, or his priestly robe. This would not have been a problem if the robe happened to come off simply because of the intensity of David's praise when he was dancing alone. But that was not the case. Apparently there were women who adorned the streets, who actually saw David in his nakedness dancing before the Lord.

This outward display on David's behalf became problematic not so much for David, but for Michal, the wife of David. There she is sitting in the palace window, awaiting her husband to return, not expecting that when she sees him coming, a harem of women would be cheering him on, absolutely enjoying David dancing naked in the street. Michal sees the women all over her man, and of course, jealousy and envy begin to exude from her insecurity. She goes into a rage, and when David arrives home, all *Hades* breaks out.

When David walks in the house, naked, and begins to explain that his nakedness came as a result of the praise dance he offered unto God, Michal became furious and said that David's nakedness had nothing to do with the Lord, but rather David had stripped naked before the women intentionally. David refuses to allow her accusations to diminish his praise unto God, and instead remains firm in his insistance that his dancing was not for the women, but it was before the Lord.

This incident became an infringement in their relationship, such that not even a steak dinner at a Ruth's Cris'

Steakhouse could resolve it. This is a crisis in the relationship. David was simply showing his love for his God, while Michal was acting on her insecurity brought to surface by the women in the street watching her husband dance. How could a love that started out so good get into this kind of position, where motives are completely misunderstood? What happened to Michal? Why is she now accusing David of misconduct when he clearly explained the motives behind his actions? What could have led to this kind of insecurity in their relationship? If we can answer these questions then we can figure out why some love relationships that have started out good, slowly become a detriment.

Michal's Relationship with the Past

Whenever we read about this incident between David and Michal, automatically bad feelings rise up toward Michal and how she became so envious of David for praising God. This would make sense if you only consider this one incident in the history of the relationship between Michal and David. But when we consider the history of hurt Michal carried with her, perhaps we may understand why she would be so bitter towards David praising God, and why the women admiring him put her in a place of insecurity.

There is an important factor to remember in the relationship between Michal and David—Michal is the daughter of

David's chief enemy, Saul. Saul desired to kill David, and when Michal discovered his intent, she lowered David out of her window in the night, and told him to stay in Naioth for a season that his life might be spared. (1 Samuel 19:12–17.)

During the wanderings of David when he was in hiding for his safety, Michal was given in marriage to Phaltiel of Gallim. (1 Samuel 25:44.) Michal apparently accepted this union without reluctance and it is evident that she gained Phaltiel's affections. Many years later, David returned home, took the throne and reclaimed Michal as his legal wife. (2 Samuel 3:13–16.) This action obviously would have put Michal in an emotional hard place. She was again legally claimed by her first husband, David, whom she obviously loved, but time and circumstances had led her to develop a love for Phaltiel as she had not expected David to come back and reclaim her. I cannot imagine the emotional toll this history must have taken on Michal.

Perhaps when Michal saw David dancing before the Lord in the presence of the women, she became angry because she knew that while her body was with David, her mind and heart were really somewhere on the other side of town with Phaltiel. Michal was dealing with some unresolved feelings and emotions. She had baggage from another relationship that she was now bringing to the celebration of David and the Ark of the Covenant.

Getting Over Past Relationships

Getting over past relationships before moving on to another relationship is very critical for the success of the new relationship. I must admit, there is always a natural tendency to remember, recall, and even relive some experiences that you have had with someone. However, those experience and memories cannot live with you in your new relationship, they must be served an eviction notice. If this radical decision to evict those old memories and move on from your past relationship does not happen, you will find yourself comparing conversations, touches, looks and even the smell of a person. Closure is a must.

> *Closure is a must.*

Closure happens when you forgive yourself for what you did in the past relationship. Many people are much too hard on themselves, and often raise questions like, "How could I be so stupid," "How could I let this happen again," or "Why is this happening to me?" These are questions that ring aloud in our ears when we have not forgiven ourselves. But think about it: You made the choices you made at the time, with information that you had, with faith in the God that you trusted. Your friends may have whispered things about your previous relationship, and perhaps you heard rumors and were given advice about the necessity of ending that relationship, but you trusted that God would make things right. Now since you've been hurt, you wonder where God was. God never left you, but He allowed you to experience certain things. Then, when you discovered that you didn't make the wisest choices, it was God who caught you, sustained you, blessed you, and is with you even while you are reading this book.

You have to forgive yourself. You didn't know that person would cheat as they did. You didn't know that they had a hidden agenda from the first time you met. You didn't know that they were not disclosing vital life changing information to you. If you would have known these things, of course you would not have engaged in relationship with them. Remind yourself of the truth that you are human, you are finite. You wanted to believe the best about that person. That was what was really in your heart, and that's true, genuine goodness. What happened, happened. Forgive yourself.

Not only do you need to forgive yourself, but it is of utmost importance that you forgive the other person. Do not misunderstand—forgiving does not mean forgetting. You may never forget the night he struck you in the face, or forget the time they left you on the side of the road in the dark of night. You may never forget how, when you returned home, all of the furniture was moved out. You may never forget some of those heart wrenching, painful, midnight hour experiences, but you can forgive.

What makes forgiveness possible? Remember these important truths:

> God had a purpose for that relationship for a season.
>
> The relationship may have hurt you,
>
> but it didn't destroy you.
>
> You can forgive, because God has forgiven you.

With these simple, yet deep spirited remembrances, forgiveness is possible.

I will never tell you that forgiveness should be a door of opportunity through which these non-appreciative people return to your life. The same God who has shown you how to truly forgive is also He who has revealed to you the true nature of these hurtful people. Now that you have this revelation, don't give them another chance to hurt you again. I once heard a talk show host say, "When people show you who they are, believe them." We try to make people into what we want them to be, but they are who they are. Embrace that truth, get over your past, and move into your future.

Loving for an Agenda Just Won't Work

When David returns with the Ark of the Covenant and dancing with joy, his wife Michal has an attitude. Perhaps not only is she bitter because she is dealing with her heart being connected with two men, but maybe she is also bitter toward

David because she knows that he only wants her for a political ploy.

According to 2 Samuel 3:12-18, Abner promises to help David become king of all Israel using the influence he possesses among the northern tribes. Abner had abandoned his allegiance to Ish-Bosheth, leader of the northern tribes and a member of Saul's household. David has now joined forces with Abner against Ish-Bosheth, to make David king of a unified Israel. But first, David must secure a wife for himself.

David could not ascend to the throne as king without a wife, so he proceeded to demand that Ish-Bosheth send Michal to be his wife again. As we mentioned previously, David had been married to Michal once, but when Saul tried to kill David and he had to flee the land for several years, while he was gone, Saul married Michal off to Paltiel as an embarrassment to David. In David's mind, if he was going to obtain the throne, he needed a wife by his side. So who does he desire? Yes, his same wife, Michal. Not because he loved her or because she was the apple of his eye, no David only wanted her because politically, she fit the bill. He had a need, and she was the answer.

Is it any wonder that Michal would be bitter because she knew she was an agenda and not a priority? It is a terrible thing for anyone you are involved with to feel like they are an agenda, and not an intricate part of your life. A person feels like they are an agenda when they are called upon only for convenience and temporary pleasure, but never recognized for things of substance and great meaning.

Agenda lovers can sense when they are an agenda and just being tolerated, hanging around for a purpose that will never be fulfilled. Agenda lovers never reach any deep engagement with their lovers, because that is not their purpose—they are just there for another person's benefit.

Most relationships today have agendas, and if you find yourself in such a situation, it is noble for you to ask yourself what the agenda of your partner might be. The agenda may be to take you for everything you have, or the agenda may be that they simply want to love you. Whatever it is, you need to know the agenda.

When you are seeking to make a wrong relationship right, it is important for you to know that people can sense when you are relating to them with an agenda on your mind. They sense when you are really not concerned about their passions, dreams, goals, and desires. When people sense that your desire for relation- *People can sense when you are relating to them with an agenda on your mind.* ship with them is driven by an agenda, they will develop feelings of isolation, which ultimately lead to a great deal of fear and frustration. So when you are seeking to establish a relationship with anyone, it is important that you evaluate your own motives. Are you in this relationship just because you want to get married or because you fear your biological clock is ticking away? Are you remaining committed because there is a great deal of money and popularity involved? Are you in the relationship because it was arranged by someone else, or is it because you really sense God is in this relationship? Is your relationship valuable to you because the two of you look good together, or is it because it makes everybody around you comfortable that you are together? Your motives should be pure, the reason for any love relationship should be love.

Perhaps Michal became so bitter because she wished David would get as excited about being around her as he was about the Ark of the Covenant. As this fleeting thought ran through her mind while she was sitting at the window watching David dance, she was again reminded that she was just part of an agenda. Loving for an agenda just won't work.

My Name Is Who I Am

We have discovered that it is possible that Michal became bitter with David because of her past or because of politics. But also it is possible that Michal became bitter because she was merely acting out a detail in her name.

Michal pronounced (mi-kal) means little stream of water, or small brook. A stream is a trinkle of water that converges with a river, then a river feeds into a canal, and finally, a canal feeds into an ocean. No doubt, the ocean is much larger than the stream, yet one is dependent on the other.

Let's make a symbolic comparison between the ocean and the stream, and David and Michal. If David's dancing in the streets because of His love for the Lord represents joy the size of the enormity of the ocean, then Michal sitting in the window with this resentment in her heart reflects spiritual fervor the size of a small stream of water. David is running over with joy, and Michal is trickling with malice and hatred.

There is a clear line of demarcation with the level of spirituality found in the two. David's spirituality reflected more of the God he served, while Michal's spirituality reflected that of her father, Saul. Remember, Saul was jealous of David because the women lifted up his name, and now Saul's daughter is jealous because women are dancing around David. Saul wanted to kill David because of his physical strength, Michal wanted to kill David because of his spiritual strength. Saul despised the anointing that David had on his life, and now it is that same anointing that has Michal in a rage. The spirit that was in Saul is now surfacing through his daughter Michal. In this case, like father, like daughter.

Small stream spirit can be described as a spirit that can't always comprehend what God is doing. It is important that when you are praying for a lover in your life, that you pray for a person who has the same capacity for God that you have. Most of the time when arguments, conflicts, fights, and confusion break out between lovers, it is because fundamentally there is an incompatibility with how they understand God to be present in their life.

I presently drive a BMW, and not long ago my battery died. I called a friend to give me a jumpstart, and after thirty minutes of trying to get my car started, nothing happened.

Later I called a tow truck, and as soon as the gentlemen connected the cable from my car to his truck, in one turn of the key, the car started immediately. I inquired of him why the jumpstart worked when I was hooked up to his truck but not when I was hooked to my friend's car. His response was, "Because the kind of car that your friend has, does not have enough voltage to get this kind of battery started. It takes more power than what he was working with."

As I was reflecting on this incident, it occurred to me that this speaks to the heart of love relationships. Whoever you are with, make sure they have enough power to jumpstart you when you breakdown. Make sure they can jumpstart you when you need mental stimulation, physical appreciation, and spiritual uplift. Because life will break you down, there is nothing like having someone who understands your capacity for God praying, cheering, and supporting you to do what God is calling you to do.

Small stream spirited people may never understand the overflow of blessings that God is bringing your way, so do not be surprised when they ask questions that are off beat, make statements that don't fit the work of the anointing, and even do things to distract you from where you need to be. Small stream lovers in many ways don't mean any harm, they just can't help that they are small, just like you can't help that you are favored to a have the Spirit of God that flows like an ocean.

What do you do if you fall in love with a small stream person, or if you have outgrown the person you are with? Notice, David never belittled Michal for where she was in her spirit. I believe that he still went to the house she lived in and blessed it. Also, he never apologized for what God did for him, nor did he hide it. When you are in love with a person who does not quite understand your dimension of God, you can't apologize. If you are married then this is a case where prayer is needed because a decision and a vow has been exchanged, and you should do all you can to make certain that your vow remains honorable. If you are single, you have a choice about whether or not you want to live the rest of your life with this small stream person. Do you always want to be in a place where you have to explain what God is doing with you, who you are, and what your passion is, or do you want to wait until God sends the destined one who can tap into you spiritually without there being much discussion about your core self at all? While searching to find the ideal, remember that oftentimes, developing relationships require work.

If you are with a small stream person, remain humble enough to pray that one day they will see God in an ocean capacity. Position yourself so that when it happens, you will be the first one they come to, to share that experience with. Be patient with them, because the truth of the matter is that all of us are a continued work of God. Making a wrong love relationship right means that you realize that God is not through with any of us yet.

LOVE RELATIONSHIP REFLECTION QUESTIONS

1. Have you ever been in love before? Describe the experience. How do you feel about that love relationship today?

2. Do you think it is possible to be in love with two people at the same time?

3. Is it possible to be in a "love relationship" and yet there be an absence of "love"?

4. Michal's life had been defined by people using her for an agenda. Have you ever felt like someone loved you with an agenda? Have you ever loved someone with an agenda?

5. Are there any past scars and bruises that you need to deal with before moving forward in another relationship?

6. How have your past experiences impacted the way you love today? Are your past experiences more of a blessing or a curse for you?

7. This chapter makes reference to Michal being "small stream" and David being "like the ocean." Have you ever been involved with a person who was incompatible with you? How did you manage the relationship?

CHAPTER 6

MAKING A WRONG
Family Relationship Right

*Saul's sons were Jonathan, Ishvi, and Malki-Shua. His
daughters were Merab, the firstborn, and Michal, the
younger. Saul's wife was Ahinoam, daughter of Ahimaaz.
Abner son of Ner was commander of Saul's army (Ner was
Saul's uncle). Kish, Saul's father, and Ner, Abner's father,
were the sons of Abiel. All through Saul's life there was
war, bitter and relentless, with the Philistines. Saul con-
scripted every strong and brave man he laid eyes on.*

I Samuel 14:49-52 MSG

This chapter will explore the possibility that the reason
that David's wife Michal could not understand the joy that
resided in his heart from the Lord, is because perhaps she was
projecting envy and jealousy on David just as she had seen her
father, Saul, do in the past. It is not unreasonable to believe
that the same spirit of malice that was in Saul, was passed
down to Michal. In other words, David and Michal's marriage

was inhibited by a generational curse that started with Saul. Every family deals with generational curses, and some very hurtful things often come as a result.

Saul's life was characterized by jealousy, insecurity, arrogance, meanness, and childishness in some ways. Saul lost his favor with God because of his disobedience and the rebellious spirit that he possessed. Because of his disobedience, it is evident that there was a curse on his life. Saul was chronically unhappy, he was discontented, he couldn't sleep at night, and he was possessed with paranoia. The curse on his life affected every relationship that Saul sought to establish, even the one with his daughter, which gives us a picture of a generational curse.

Curses are real, and they have the capacity of reaching and affecting other generations of people who are in the lineage of the one who is carrying the curse. I do not believe that there is a family in existence today that is not affected by some generational curses. If generational blessings are real, then generational curses are real. There are times when a curse can be present though lying dormant, and then something happens in your life that will bring the curse to surface and it is then that you discover that you are dealing with a generational curse.

Relationships are affected by curses.

Relationships are affected by curses. A curse can cause a person to put up a wall, become paranoid, promiscuous, shy, bitter, suspicious, an over-achiever, or a workaholic. Curses have caused people to have insomnia, lose hair, break out in hives, have a nervous stomach, and even experience unhealthy weight loss or gain. Consider for a moment some of the generational curses that affect family relationships.

The Curse of Incest

Sheila falls to sleep on the couch in the front room. It is the middle of the night when she feels a hand rubbing the side of her leg and then suddenly, there are lips on her lips. She is startled and opens her eyes only to discover that it is her father who has a grip on her face, forcing her to kiss him back. Sheila has just been the victim of incest.

Incestuous relationships can be described as any sensual or sexual relationship between closely related members of a family. It is not a natural thing for a family member to desire another family member. This is a sickness and certainly an abomination before God as mentioned in Leviticus 18:6 and 20:12. Those who induce you to commit yourself to an incestuous relationship will try to make you think that it is alright, and that you must keep it a secret. Incest is a violation of boundaries. It involves touching, kissing, gazing in the eyes, sexual expression, and even erotic emotional communication. These expressions should not take place with another family member for it is indeed a clear defiance of God's plan and a curse upon the generations.

The Curse of Verbal and Emotional Abuse

Victor is doing everything he can to stay focused in school. While he acknowledges the need to get a good education and make good grades, it is difficult for him to perform because of his reality at home. When he gets home from school, his mother greets him at the door reeking of alcohol. The slurred words released from her lips cut deep as she tells Victor, "You are stupid! You will never make anything of your life! I hate you because you look too much like your father!"

This is a clear case of verbal abuse and emotional abuse. This kind of abuse affects behavior, self-esteem, future aspirations, eating habits, composure, and even behavior towards others.

The Curse of Incompletion

Krystal is gifted in so many areas, and is a master at starting entrepreneurial projects. She beams with excitement while doing things she really enjoys. She is organized, has all plans on paper, and has made networking contacts. However, when the curse of incompletion rears its head soon after she starts executing her plan, she get to a point where she experiences a block. She loses the zeal and the passion that is needed to see the project through. As a matter of fact, she looks back over her life and realizes that her mother never finished anything she started. Her father spent a lifetime starting jobs and then quitting them for no apparent reason. Her brother has had multiple relationships, none of which ever amounted to anything. Krystal notices that everyone in her family wrestles with completing what they start.

This is an example of the curse of incompletion. This curse does not allow a person to complete a process, they are easily distracted and fail to finish. It is the enemy's intent to stop the destiny of God from coming forth. Starting an effort and not finishing is evidence of the curse of incompletion.

The Curse of Sexual Addiction

Denise was the shining star of the church. She grew up getting all of the lead roles in the church plays, she led most of the songs in the choir, as a teenager she even represented the church at the state convention. However, while at one of the conventions she attended when she was 15, a young man who was 19 took advantage of her in the hotel swimming pool.

For years after being raped in the pool, Denise never breathed a word of this encounter. She never told anyone because of the fear that she would get in trouble, she would get blamed, or it would affect her father's job because he was the pastor. Denise kept this bottled up inside, deciding the way she would cope with it was by making the decision to have another sexual encounter, hoping that it would erase the memory of the rape. What she discovered instead was that while she felt valued for a while, as soon as she would get comfortable and think she was over the trauma, that guy would leave her.

She finds herself in a vicious cycle of moving from relationship to relationship, thinking that another sexual relationship will make her forget about the pain. Denise becomes addicted to the feeling of escape while having sex, so at age 30, she finds herself using sex to cover up the pain of a rape that happened when she was 15.

While dealing with this addiction, Denise meets a young man named Demond who has the same addiction. After they are married for four years, they find themselves sharing their secrets. She talks about her rape, and he mentions that he too had been violated by an uncle. Demond confides that ever since he was violated, he has been trying to recover his masculinity through sex.

Both Denise and Demond enter into counseling, and they discover that their sexual addictions are rooted in their past. Though the counseling helps, they both remain very insecure about their child ever being out of their presence, for fear that what happened to them will happen to their child. They refuse to have this curse passed down to the next generation. Their willingness to be real with themselves and each other about this curse allowed them to confront it.

The Curse of Alcoholism and Drugs

Charles is wonderful father to his children and a caring husband to his wife. He works a regular job, and is a Sunday School teacher at the church. However, Charles is wrestling with the demon of alcoholism, which keeps him drinking at night after working during the day. He has gone to many counselors and has even spoken to his pastor about this matter. What he has discovered is that what he is dealing with as a man, started as a seed when he was just a boy.

As a boy, Charles watched his father drink with his uncles. Charles' first time getting drunk was in college, where it soon became a nightly activity for him. Drinking has had a grip on his life that he just can't shake, however it didn't occur to him that it was a generational curse until he found himself tempting his oldest son to taste of a mixed drink. When his son refused, Charles became hostile and angry, and it was then that he saw himself transferring his curse to the next generation.

Alcoholism and drug abuse affects family relationships, not to mention the deterioration it causes to one's health. One way a family is affected by alcohol and drug abuse is that they do not know what to expect from the abuser. The abuser can't be counted on to keep his commitments, either within the family or outside. This forces families to lie and cover up for failures of their loved one. It forces them, in some ways, to live in a world of denial. Alcohol and drug abuse within a family also leaves family members with a sense of insecurity. Drug users often steal, find themselves wanted by the police, and at times even do drugs or hide them in their own house. This places the entire family in danger. The biggest misconception of this curse is that the person who is drinking or drugging is only hurting themselves. Not so. Everybody who cares for the abuser, who has to live with them and nurture them, is hurt while they watch their loved one ultimately destroy himself.

The Curse of Negative Thinking

Valencia is never pleased with anything. She is critical with people on her job, in her sorority, and in her church. If there is not a problem, she will create one while using that opportunity to address a host of other concerns. Valenica is not only critical of others, but she is even critical of herself. She is a perfectionist and falls apart if anything happens that is out of her control.

One day, one of Valencia's cousins, in a moment of rage, said, "Valencia you are so negative, just like your mother!" Humbled, Valencia goes to her mother and asks her mother why was she like this. Her mother responds by saying, "I only say the things to you that my mother said to me, and if you can't handle it, you need to grow up."

The curse of negative thinking is probably one of the easiest curses to be transferred through the generations because it is so easy to repeat what has been said to you. The mind acts like a recorder. In our minds, we play back what we read, hear, and see. Valencia was simply acting out what she had experienced all her life. The fact of the matter is, if she doesn't get a hold on this situation and end this generational curse, her daughter one day will be the victim of negative thinking, too.

The Curse of Narcissim

The word "narcissim" has a very interesting history. In Roman mythology, there is the story of a handsome young man by the name of Narcissus who rejected a nymph named Echo. Heartbroken, Echo cried out to Venus asking for revenge upon Narcissus. Venus granted this petition for revenge and caused Narcissus to fall in love with his own reflection in a pool of water. Once Narcissus realized that he had fallen in love with his own reflection and that the reflection would never be able to reciprocate his love, he wasted away, despondent.[1]

Narcissim is manifested by being consumed with self. Many people are affected by narcissm. There are parents who do not pour into their children because they are consumed with themselves. There are couples that never reach a good place in the relationship because one is constantly concerned about himself.

Paul was a nice guy to Jasmin, but things never progressed because Paul was selfish with his time, he never wanted to share what he had, and every activity centered around him. Jasmin asked if she could taste Paul's dessert at dinner once and he simply said, "Get your own." On more than one occasion when both of them went shopping, more time was spent looking for things for Paul than for Jasmin, and in fact, he was ready to leave the mall when it was time to shop for her. While sitting in the park on a lunch date that Jasmin set up, it started raining. Paul got up, took his belongings, and ran quickly to the car so that he wouldn't get wet, while Jasmin got drenched gathering the cooler, the blanket, and the food that they partially ate.

Paul is presenting for us a picture of narcissim, but what Jasmin would discover in a future conversation with Paul's mother is that he was not the first generation in his family to carry this trait. Paul's mother would advise, "Don't worry about Paul being selfish, he is just like his father and his other brothers. They all look out for themselves." His mother went on with a nod of her head, "So baby, you need to learn how to look out for you, because my son will probably never change."

Other Family Curses

There is good news, however. There is a way to break generational curses to make wrong family relationships, right.

There are many other generational curses we could discuss—adultery, pornography, homosexuality, fear of failure, fear of rejection, double-mindedness, lying, stealing, rage, bitterness, arrogance, gossiping, prejudice, racism, suicide, denial—the list seems almost overwhelming and certainly much too long for us to detail in this work. There is good news, however. There is a way to break generational curses to make wrong family relationships, right.

Find the Cycle

Finding the cycle of a generational curse can be done by simply analyzing the history of your family, looking to find a pattern that is evident even in your own life. Finding the cycle requires honesty and commitment to really ask the hard questions about your family and your life. This requires asking questions like,

Why am I the way I am?

What are some of the things in my family that I believe are dysfunctional?

What are the triggers that allow my alter-ego to come forth?

Who else in my family behaves in this manner?

Finding the cycle is about identifying the area of concern and really seeing it for what it is.

Break the Silence

Breaking the silence means that you get to a point in your journey where you feel comfortable enough to share your story with someone confidentially. It is the adversary's desire that you keep your "secret" a secret, however, sharing your story with someone like a counselor, pastor, or even a medical doctor can you help as you hear yourself acknowledge the cycle of behavior while also gathering some allies to help you as you fight to break the curse. There is a risk to breaking the silence, but the strength you can gain from the support of another far outweighs the risk. I would rather you yell in concert with somebody else, than suffer in silence. Get it out, and get it off of you. There will be a season where you will feel guilty for even sharing, but know that this is the first step to healing and after awhile the guilt will dissipate.

Eat Daily Bread

Jesus taught His disciples to pray, *Give us this day our daily bread* (Matthew 6:11). Some scholars believe that when Jesus mentioned this, He was making reference to God providing manna for Israel on a daily basis. The key word in this interpretation is "daily." God intends for you to feed yourself inspiration, validation, positive thoughts, and His Word on a daily basis. He has made daily provisions of these items for you to partake. Every day you have to fight against the temptation to recall negative moments in your life, and make up in your mind that you are the one in the family who will break the cycle. In order to have strength for this task, you must take the provision of daily bread that God provides.

Prepare for Attack

When you break the silence about your violation or the cycle that exists in your family, look for the family to "hush" you. Not everybody in the family will be ready for the secret to be revealed. Never would I suggest that you willingly bring embarrassment to your family, but at this point you must speak so that you can have life. Part of the "curse" is the drive to keep covering it up, which sets the next generation in place to repeat it. You may find that you are no longer invited to the family dinner, loved ones may heap shame and assault on your character to deflect from the real issue, you may even risk losing some friends who may not want to be affiliated or identified with you after you give this revelation. Prepare for the attack, but never forget that God built you to handle it. If you handled the violation that you experienced, then, with God's help, you can handle anything.

Forgive

After you have gone through the previously mentioned steps, there has to be a time in the process when you willingly forgive. Every day you live holding on to the pain of the violation or the "secret" you continue to give the curse hurricane force strength. Through the power of Christ, we must learn to forgive. In forgiving people, you must also forgive yourself. Though what has happened to you was not your fault, there may still be some guilt you are carrying that you must forgive. Forgiving is about healing, restoration, revitalization, and a new direction for you. You deserve forgiveness so that you can have joy in your spirit. Joy comes when we forgive.

You Have Permission to "Curse"

When Jesus was traveling on his way to Calvary, He stopped at a fig tree along the side of the road. When Jesus saw that the fig tree was not bearing fruit, the Bible tells us that Jesus cursed the tree, and the tree could no longer bear fruit.

The curse that continues to haunt your family is like the fig tree that is not bearing any fruit. It is time for you to curse the curse. Now don't be confused, "cursing" is not the same as "cussing." "Cussing" involves uttering expletives that, while they may help vent your anger, do not prove useful or helpful in dealing with the root problem. Cussing has no power. But when you "curse," you call on the Name that is above every other name, you plead the blood, you speak those thing that are not as though they were. When you curse the curse, you declare that this curse ends with you, and it shall not be found in the next generation. You not only have permission to curse, but as a child of God, He gives you authority to curse the curse.

FAMILY RELATIONSHIP
REFLECTION QUESTIONS

1. David's family was inundated with trickery, deception, and drama. Is there anything in your family that may resemble this kind of family dynamic?

2. This chapter speaks of the reality of generational curses. After reading the various curses in this chapter, which of these can you identify with in your family experience?

3. Once you have identified the curse that is in your family, what do you belive is the best way to address this critical matter?

4. What are some of the goals you have for your family as you build relationships with one another?

5. What are some of the family traits you celebrate about your family? What are some areas that your family needs to pray about?

6. The last section of this chapter speaks of forgiving. Who in your family do you need to forgive so that your relationship with them can be made right?

CHAPTER 7

MAKING A WRONG
Social Networking
Relationship Right

*They brought the Chest of GOD and set it in the middle
of the tent pavilion that David had pitched for it. Then
and there David worshiped, offering burnt offerings and
peace offerings. When David had completed the sacrifices
of burnt and peace offerings, he blessed the people in the
name of GOD-of-the-Angel-Armies and handed out to
each person in the crowd, men and women alike, a loaf of
bread, a date cake, and a raisin cake. Then everyone
went home.*

2 Samuel 6:17–19 MSG

We are living in a day when social networking is popular.
However, the social networking relationships of facebook™,
MySpace™, twitter™, e-mail and texting must be put into
perspective with relationships that really matter. It is vital that
we not lose sight of the fact that our relationship with God is

much more important than our race to gain social admirers. This chapter will talk about the pros and cons of using technology to relate, and how to keep social interaction in perspective. We will also discuss healthy and unhealthy social environments, and how to detect when people are compatible with your level of socializing.

When David brought the Ark of the Covenant back home, the Bible declares that he broke out dancing until he danced out of his robe. The dance that David was performing is a dance called the Malawayi.[1] When dancing the Malawayi, one dances on the left foot and spins around in circles. This is the dance that David performed every six steps once he received the Ark of the Covenant back in his presence. It is interesting to me that David chose a dance that requires him to dance on his left foot. The left side is traditionally viewed as the side of weakness and failure. It is almost as if David is saying, "God I know that I have failed You by putting more emphasis on the death of my friend Uzzah than I have You. I know that I was weak and gave into anger towards You and decided to leave the Ark of the Covenant at Obed-Edom's house. I know I messed up sorely in Your eyes, so God if I have to, I will praise You on my left leg, to show how unworthy I am." Even though David may not have felt worthy, he still realized that God is worthy to be praised.

Not only was David dancing in circles on his left leg, but he was also offering a sacrifice to God every six steps. This means that when David was dancing in the streets, he was dancing on the blood of oxen, fatlings, and other animals that were being sacrificed to God. To bring this into modern day perspective, I have to ask—Church, when are we going to stop dancing and praising God for houses, cars, new suits and shoes, iPods, and flat screen T.V.'s, and learn how to bless God simply for the blood of Jesus?

David is so consumed in his praise dance, that he dances himself out of his robe. Not even the women who were admiring the nakedness of David nor the accusations or his wife would stop him from offering his praise. David ignored their admiration to remain passionate about his worship before God. It did not matter if the women looked lustfully at David, he made it clear at that moment that the only relationship that mattered to him was his relationship with God.

What is noteworthy to me is that when David was dancing, his mind and spirit were not focused on the many admirers that he had among the women and the many relationships that he could have formed. His mind was set on God. This message should speak to so many people today, because many of our relationships are void of God. Our relationship with God is an afterthought, at best.

A prevalent trend in our culture today is for relationships to be developed without knowing anything of substance about the person with whom you are developing a relationship. A person can become your "friend" with the click of a button. They log on and read intimate information on your facebook™ page, and yet never meet you face to face. We are living in a day when

Social networking technology has impacted our theology of God.

blogging has become a popular form of communication, while skyping™ is allowing people to come right into your home through a web cam. Text messaging has become the communication method of choice for so many families and friends, which gives us every reason not to talk to one another face to face. I'm not suggesting that you can't have technology and God, but I am absolutely convinced that social networking technology has impacted our theology of God. Therefore, I think it is important that we take a moment and consider how social networking sites impact the relationships that we develop.

facebook™

In the past few years, a social networking phenomenon has hit our landscape like no other before it—the phenomenon is called facebook™. One Tuesday night on the campus of Harvard University, a young sophomore by name of Mark Zuckerberg broke up with a girlfriend, and while trying to find something to occupy his mind, Mark came up with "facemash" or what is more affectionately known today as facebook™.

Facebook™ is a social networking website that has 400 million people logging on. Facebook™ has allowed many people to reconnect with old relationships. It has served as a platform for individuals to express themselves, and has served as a marketing venue for businesses, churches, and nonprofit organizations. Facebook™ has also served as a way to announce weddings, funerals, class reunions, share family photos, birth announcements and other interesting events. *Entertainment Weekly* put it on its end-of-the-decade "best-of" list, saying, "How on earth did we stalk our exes, remember our co-workers' birthdays, bug our friends, and play a rousing game of Scrupulous before Facebook?"[2]

While facebook™ has contributed to many people establishing relationships, I believe it is incumbent on the Church to point out that not all facebook™ relationships have been good, and the concept of relationship that facebook™ proliferates can lead one to develop a bad and even harmful relationship.

THE THEOLOGY OF FACEBOOK™

When I speak of the theology of facebook™, I'm talking about understanding facebook™ from a God perspective. This is not to suggest that we know exactly what God is thinking, but looking at facebook™ from a God perspective can help illuminate how facebook™ can become a hinderance to our relationship with God if we are not careful.

CAN I BE YOUR FRIEND?

The predominant feature of facebook™, is the interaction between "friends." This "friend" idea was not put in place by accident. When we consider the term "friend" in light of the inception of this website, it makes perfect sense. Mark Zuckerberg created facebook™ at a time when he needed a friend. His girlfriend had just dropped him, and if there was anything he felt could help him get over her, it would have been another friend. In other words, this social website was created out of a need for a friend. Thus today we have 400 million people who spend most of their day looking for "friends" with whom they can connect and develop some kind of relationship.

The point of concern around looking for a friend on facebook™ is that, in some ways, it reduces tremendously the value of a friend. There was a time when the word "friend" had great meaning and value. It was a label that was only applied in relationships that were proven and tested. Henry David Thoreau put it best when he said, "The language of friendship is not words but meanings." The truth is, not everybody is qualified to be called your friend. A friend is someone who will be there for you through thick and thin. A friend will support you when others fail you. A friend will tell you the truth, even when it is not popular to do so. A friend will challenge you to be the best you can be, and will not be envious or jealous when you succeed. A friend will not judge you for where you are, but will always see what you have the potential of becoming.

Not everybody is qualified to be called your friend.

Friends truly are very difficult to come by, however, facebook™ has made it seem very simple. All you have to do is click a button. Our perception of facebook™ may not be so much about Mark Zuckerberg's broken relationship as it is about our broken relationship with ourself. What does the need to have over 300 friends on your profile say about you, particularly when Proverbs 18:24 declares, *The man of many friends [a friend of all the world] will prove himself a bad friend, but there is a friend who sticks closer than a brother* (AMP). To say that you are a "bad friend" does not mean that you are a bad person, it just means that, from a biblical perspective, there is much more involved with becoming a friend than a click of the button. Friendship is about loyalty, sacrifice, accountability and respect. If all 300 of your "friends" on your profile can prove themselves to you in this way, by all means, call them your friend. But if by chance they cannot, are they really your friend?

If you are searching for a friend, know that Christ is the best friend you could ever have. In addition, please don't think I sound more heavenly bound than earthly good when I tell you that the Spirit of Christ will also lead you to friends if you ask Him to do so. Yes, some great things can happen via technology, specifically via facebook™, but even on facebook™ , allow the Spirit of God to lead you and help you to discern who is the right friend for you.

PLEASE ACCEPT ME?

Another noteworthy issue with the way the facebook™ system is set up concerns the actual process you must go through to become a member of someone's "friend" list. Once you identify a person you know or you would like to know, in order to become that person's "friend," you must ask them if they will accept you as their friend. If they accept you, then you're in the group and you have access to their entire facebook™ world. Hooray! But what about if they do not accept you? What if they click "ignore" on your request to be accepted?

Perhaps the genesis of this "acceptance" thing had its roots in the fact that Mark Zuckerburg, who developed facebook™, did so at a time in his life when he felt like his girlfriend didn't accept him. He had just been dumped. For people who feel like they have been dumped all of their lives, never able to be successful in a relationship, never fully appreciated or affirmed by anyone, those words "accepted" must have tremendous value, even if they're coming from a "friend" that you may not even know. To be accepted is a great thing, but you must keep in context by whom you are being accepted.

Some of the people we are accepting on facebook™ may be people whom perhaps we don't need to accept. For example, there may be a person from your past with whom you had a toxic relationship. You may have escaped from that relationship many years before, but all it takes is a few clicks on facebook™ and that person is again knocking at your door, requesting to be your friend. Once you accept them, the communication starts all over again. At the time, it may seem like an innocent gesture, I mean, you wouldn't want to ignore their request, would you? But on another, spiritual, level, this may be a way that the enemy is trying to reintroduce you to someone God has already delivered you from. Before you know it, a facebook™ conversation results in a face to face interaction. Now all the drama, cheating, fussing and fighting you have been delivered from for ten years is back, all because of a simple click of the button. Your innocent "acceptance" has put you in that vicious cycle again.

Be on your guard—do not allow your need for acceptance to put you in the position of accepting harmful influences in your life that God once delivered you from. God presently has you on another highway. Stay there. You are accepted by God when you make Christ your Savior, and when Christ accepts you, know who you are apart from facebook™. You are the Lord's child and you are wonderfully made in the image of God.

PICTURE THIS

What really makes facebook™ a drawing place for millions is the fabulous and sometimes bizarre pictures and personal information that you are able to explore. While it is always nice to show the world how beautiful or handsome you are, there have been many people who have gotten in trouble because of pictures and personal information they chose to post on their facebook™ page.

It is absolutely imperative that you limit what you publish on your facebook™ profile. Perhaps one of the most extreme cases involving failure to properly limit information on a profile came to light on March 4, 2010, when the Israeli Defense forces had to call off a raid against Palestinian militants in the West Bank when they discovered that one of their soldiers posted on his facebook™ page, "On Wednesday we are cleaning out the village of Katana (or Ramallah)—today and arrest operation, tomorrow an arrest operation and then please god, home by Thursday."[3] You may say that you're not doing anything as careless as doling out information on pending military actions, but even for everyday citizens, it is important that you limit the amount of information you put out there. Many workplaces, universities, and other agencies are now using facebook™ postings to get a sense of your character, interactions, and the quality of company you keep.

With this in mind, we need to ask, what material is appropriate for posting on a Christian's facebook™ page? How much should be revealed? What avenues are appropriate for circulating this type of information? How can you safeguard yourself and your character from any fraud or malicious practices? These are just a few questions that need to be considered, therefore consider the following observations that follow as a guide for having a facebook™ relationship.

How to Make a Wrong Facebook Relationship Right

Your facebook™ page should not contain any information that reveals your personal residence address, work location, daily routine, schedule, family dialogue, or details of personal conflicts you recently had.

A Christian's facebook™ page should not contain pictures that do not represent Christ and His kingdom appropriately. It should not contain photos of a sensual or explicit nature, social pictures in which you are perceived as drinking or smoking, or photos that would show you in a compromising position.

Use of facebook™ by a Christian should not include words that foster gossip or slander. Personal insults and attacks should not be found on your profile.

A Christian's facebook™ page should represent good character and reflect the high standards that you possess as a child of God. Along this line, you must also be cautious even about who you accept as a friend. Remember, when you accept someone as your friend, their pictures and information will eventually reflect back on you.

Blogs

Another new age form of communication is called blogging. Originally referred to as a "weblog" by Jorn Barger, we can thank Peter Merholz for shortening the term simply to "blog." A blog is a commentary tool which allows people to virtually publish their opinions about a given subject matter. These blogs do not have to be based in fact, they are simply platforms for opinions and insights given by people who can choose to remain anonymous, who are not required to cite their credentials or qualifications for holding forth on the matter in question. The potential danger in this form of commentary is obvious—a person reading the blog may mistakenly count information as being factual or true when, in fact, it may not be.

While blogging provides a platform for freedom of expression, it has also served as a stumbling block to many people politically, socially, and even financially. In 2006, Mark Cuban, owner of the Dallas Mavericks, criticized NBA officials on the court, and then posted defamatory comments on his blog page. He was fined heavily for those actions. Delta Airlines fight attendant Ellen Simonetti was fired from her job because she posted pictures of herself in uniform on her blog "Queen of Sky: Diary of a Flight Attendant." Jessica Cutler, while working as a congressional assistant, blogged about her sex life on her blog "The Washingtonienne." She is currently being sued by one of her former lovers for failure to protect his right to privacy.

At the time of this writing, I can personally speak to the danger of irresponsible blogging as my family and my ministry have suffered a personal blog attack. The issue centers around unfair treatment directed toward my family while dining at a local restaurant. This restaurant was enforcing their 18% tip surcharge policy, published to only be assessed to parties of 6 or more, against parties of fewer than 6 people—in some cases, when there were as few as only 3 diners in the party. When we sought to bring this matter to the attention of the management along with other issues, we were rebuffed. We notified the media of these unfair practices and the media opted to produce a story on this issue. When the media outlet interviewed the restaurant owner, he said that he assessed this unfair charge because a member of my family was a "bad tipper." While this accusation could not be further from the truth, this was the catch phrase that would ultimately have media outlets such as CNN, MSNBC, ABC, The Tom Joyner Morning Show, and countless others discussing this issue of a restaurant having the right to enforce a tip on people who dine.

Along with this legitimate discussion of tipping policy enforcement came unwarranted blogs from people who were servers in restaurants who used my family member as a target to vent their frustration about people who eat in their restaurants and don't leave a tip. While my family member has always been a good tipper, that reality was now lost in the mass of words issued in anger—words which were not true, tested, or substantiated. The character of my family member was unfairly maligned by people who have never met her, seen her or even know the truth about the story at the heart of this firestorm.

The point of the story was lost amid the slander. The story was not about someone being a bad tipper, the story was about how, in the state of North Carolina a restaurant owner is not required to pay a server at least minimum wage of $7.25

an hour, but is instead allowed to pay them only $2.13 an hour. Only if the server does not make any tips within that hour, does the restaurant owner, by law, have to pay that server the difference to raise their pay up to $7.25 for that hour. What this leads to is restaurant owners who will extort money in any way possible, including adding unpublished tip surcharges to tickets, to get more money from the guest to ensure that the extra money does not have to come out of the restaurant's till. Should any restaurant patron call foul on the addition of unpublicized tip surcharges, the owner's response is simply to label that patron a "bad tipper."

Into the midst of this messy, convoluted situation and many others just like this one, steps bloggers—anonymous, uninformed bloggers—who oftentimes throw their opinions out to the general public, cloaking them as fact when they are not.

Interesting Facts About These Blogs

In our personal experience with the dangers of blogging, we found that the blogs gave people a chance to voice their discontent who, though not directly involved in the situation at hand, harbored jealousy toward our ministry. Though our ministry is known in the community for supporting community programs, transforming the lives of the "least of these" and holding high moral standards of excellence, the blog system gave these haters a venue to express opinions about the kingdom of God that had nothing to do with the story. The blog system became an outlet for scores of anonymous people to talk about anything but the issue. This becomes the real problem with blogging—since you don't know who is saying what, it is nearly impossible to verify whether or not the information is valid.

These are serious acts of defamation of character, and many people never find out who is actually doing it. Some, however, have chosen to take a stand against such defamations at the hand of bloggers. By May 2009, $17.4 million in damages had been awarded in defamation suits linked to blogging.[4]

Though it is an uphill battle to unmask these anonymous bloggers, steps have been taken in this direction. In *Doe v. Cahill*, by a strange twist, the Delaware Supreme Court allowed the injured parties—the Cahill's—to obtain the identity of John Doe, who turned out to be one of Councilman Cahill's political rivals. Unfortunately, most people will never have the chance to discover the identity of the one who has slandered them and will just have to live with the pain. Perhaps President Barak Obama summed it up best when he stated, "If the direction of the news is all blogosphere, all opinions, with no serious fact-checking, no serious attempts to put stories in context, then what you will end up getting is people shouting at each other across the void but not a lot of mutual understanding."[5]

The Theology of the Blog

In the book of Genesis, Adam and Eve fall victim to false information presented as true. Satan falsely represented to

Adam and Eve that what God had spoken of the tree of knowledge was not necessarily true. Satan made them believe that they could eat from the tree, and no harm would come upon them. Adam and Eve did eat, and sin and death became humankind's ultimate fate. However, in the final analysis of this story, it is obvious that Adam and Eve's sin was not so much that they ate the fruit, the sin was that they believed what was told to them by the serpent rather than believe God. They put more confidence in what the serpent said, rather than trusting what God said. Just like a nefarious blogger, Satan plants the seed and then slowly goes behind the curtain of anonymity, leaving Adam, Eve, and humanity holding the bag.

> *They put more confidence in what the serpent said, rather than trusting what God said.*

This notion of blogging with its ability to spread a rumor unjustifiably, takes grace and mercy to a whole new level. With it now so easy for someone to blog and plant seeds of suspicion in churches, marriages, dating relationships, friendships, and even business acquaintances, every day you live and your name has not been blogged, you should thank God for His grace and mercy.

Proverbs 22:1 says, *A good name is rather to be chosen than great riches, and loving favour rather than silver and gold.* The writer indicates that favor is attached to a good name. If someone slanders your good name in a blog, it is reasonable to assume that you will lose favor in the eyes of some people.

Sadly, human nature shows that some people believe things even if they prove not to be true. Therefore, you must understand your value and where that value comes from if you find yourself the victim of a blog. Do those people who are blogging about you really know you? Do they have any knowledge about the destiny God has prepared for your life? Do these strangers know what God has whispered in your ear about what He is ready to do with your life? You are blessed and destined for promotion—now let them go and blog that!

HOW TO MAKE A WRONG BLOGGING RELATIONSHIP RIGHT

- Christians should never blog any information that is going to be damaging to the kingdom of God. Remember every time you blog and put a fellow Christian in bad light, you are also blogging against the name of Christ.

- If you have ever put any false information about someone on any blogging website, you owe it to the individual to retract your statement and do everything possible to make it right.

- Make certain that any information you post in a blog can be proven true and that it is indeed factual. If you would not be willing to post something under your own name, perhaps you shouldn't post it. Always keep in mind that you could be sued for slander.

- When you are blogging, don't give in to the temptation to lose sight of the reality that you are writing about real human beings who were made in the image of God. You are writing about a person who has a family, they may have children, and most importantly, they may be a fellow Christian. The fundamental question that you should raise is, *Would I want this said about me, if the tables were turned?*

The Theology of Skyping

Skyping is a new technology experience that really makes the world smaller. Skyping enables you to carry on a long-distance conversation while you actually see a person on your computer monitor and they see your image on their monitor as it is transmitted through your web cam. Skyping can strengthen relationships because it allows you to see the person you are talking to rather than just hear a voice. Skyping is such a fun experience that it can actually become quite addictive.

Imagine what would happen if you would take a moment to skype™ with God.

How to Make a Wrong Skyping Relationship Right

If you are going take time to skype™ a friend to stay in touch, imagine what would happen if you would take a moment to skype™ with God. Skyping with God means that you take a moment and see God face to face. You and God have a conversation while looking at one another. Matthew 6:32-33 tells us, *For after all these things do the Gentiles seek: for your heavenly Father knoweth that ye have need of these things. But seek ye first the kingdom of God and his righteousness; and all these things shall be added unto you.* There is so much to chase after in this world and technology often complicates more than simplifies our lives. But God wants your attention. It is this kind of invasion into your private life that God has been waiting to have with you for a while. Relax and let it happen. You will be amazed what God will tell you when you spend time skyping with Him.

The Theology of Twittering

There is a very popular phenomenon sweeping the globe called twitter™. Twitter™ is a social networking micro-blogging service created by Jack Dorsey in 2006. Tweets are text based messages posted on an author's page with the words being delivered to the followers of the author. For instance, if a person wants to know what the day has been like for a celebrity, they can subscribe to that celebrity's tweets. The celebrity tweets brief details of their daily activities which are sent out to all subscribers, and the people who are following the celebrity feel connected to that person and in some ways feel that they enter into their intimate personal lives. Celebrities may tweet about brushing their teeth, how they are wearing their hair that day, what they are eating for dinner, or whose movie they are working on or whose song they are recording. It is possible that a celebrity would have hundreds and thousands of followers.

The important thing to remember about tweeting is to keep it in perspective. Remember that when someone is communicating to you on a mass level, you are a part of a mass following. Also keep in mind that these kinds of social networking tools can be addictive. Monitor how much time you spend doing this in a day. Is most of your time spent on activities like this or is it spent on more meaningful things?

By His Word and His Spirit, God sends us daily tweets.

In considering the theology of twitter™, let us think of how, by His Word and His Spirit, God sends us daily tweets. There are intimate details about God's nature and character that we are invited to discover each day. God is looking for followers who desire to subscribe to His daily tweets given through His Word and Spirit. Are you a follower of Christ? Then tune into what God is communicating and allow that information to make you a more passionate follower of Him.

How to Make a Wrong Twittering Relationship Right

Making a wrong twitter™ relationship right starts with knowing the value that you have in the eyes of God. He wants to spend time with you. Just as we expect "face time" with those who are important to us, God is expecting the same from us. God has promised us that, *The LORD also will be a refuge for the oppressed, a refuge in times of trouble. And they that know thy name will put their trust in thee: for thou, LORD, hast not forsaken them that seek thee* (Psalm 9:9-10).

While social networking can be very positive, I believe that God is more interested in us networking with Him and the things connected to His kingdom. If social networking is your way of filling a void in your life, know that God is able to fill that void through His Word. Christ is a friend who sticks closer than a brother. (Proverbs 18:24.) Network with Him, and you will be fine!

SOCIAL NETWORKING RELATIONSHIP REFLECTION QUESTIONS

1. How important is it for you to have social networking sites as a means for building relationships in your life?

2. Do you believe the Internet services and social networking sites are a blessing or a curse to our culture today?

3. How has skyping, blogging, and twittering benefited your spiritual walk with God?

4. Have you or someone you know had their reputation or character attacked on any social networking sites?

5. Facebook™ introduces the idea of you accepting "friends" to be a part of your networking chain. What is your definition of a real friend? Do you think that facebook™ has devalued what it means to have a friend in your life?

6. Do you believe that blogging is a fair system for sharing information? What do you think about idea of people being allowed to make statements anonymously?

7. What are some positive ways people can use social networking sites to establish healthy relationships?

CHAPTER 8

MAKING A WRONG
Sexual Relationship Right

One late afternoon, David got up from taking his nap and was strolling on the roof of the palace. From his vantage point on the roof he saw a woman bathing. The woman was stunningly beautiful. David sent to ask about her, and was told, "Isn't this Bathsheba, daughter of Eliam and wife of Uriah the Hittite?" David sent his agents to get her. After she arrived, he went to bed with her. (This occurred during the time of "purification" following her period.) Then she returned home. Before long she realized she was pregnant. Later she sent word to David: "I'm pregnant."

2 Samuel 11: 2–5 MSG

After coming through so much to finally become king of Israel and to see the Ark of the Covenant returned to the city of Jerusalem, it is hard to believe that David would put himself into the position to fall into an adulterous sexual relationship with Bathsheba. Let us explore how the lust of the flesh could make David forget his reverence for God and His Spirit, and focus only on satisfying himself. But in this discussion, let us remember that this improper sexual relationship was not the end of David's story. Just as David turned his situation around by making good choices in obedience to the Word of God, we will see that there is hope for those who have likewise made some bad sexual decisions and have developed some worldly sexual ties. If God could return David to right standing, He assures us that anybody who puts their trust in Him has the privilege to return to a life of purity. In the hopes that we can help others avoid falling into the trap of lust in the first place, we will also discuss the stages of dating and suggest godly activities to engage in while in a dating relationship.

Who Is a Sex Addict?

When we think about the mighty warrior David, the king of Israel, the one who was described as a man after God's own heart, it is hard to then think about him as having an issue with sexual discipline. Sexual addictions are real. The National Council on Sexual Addiction and Compulsivity has defined sexual addiction as a persistent and escalating pattern of sexual behaviors acted out despite increasing negative consequences to self or others. Sex addicts do not just enjoy the pleasure of sex, they are out of control and have lost the ability to limit their sexual behaviors. Their behavior has spiraled out of control to the point where sex is no longer about pleasure, but about compulsion and pain. Sex is now used as a means of escape, a stress reliever, or as something to occupy the time that is unfulfilled. Sex can be as addictive as any drug.

Sex can be as addictive as any drug.

Many people do not consider themselves to be sex addicts because, unlike a crack addict, cocaine addict or alcoholic, you can be a sex addict without anyone knowing it because your physical features don't give testimony to your addiction. Sex addicts dress up when they come to church, wear nice professionally tailored clothing to work, and get their hair and nails done in upscale facilities. They may even have spouses and families that never know of their addictions. But just because their addictions may not be apparent to the eye, make no mistake, sexual addictions are real, and this elicit spirit has its way of manifesting in ways and in people like you would never imagine.

Such is the case with David, who finds himself in a situation that looks all too much like one you might find in a person who is suffering from a sex addiction. This disasterous chain of events all started when David decided not to join his troops in battle, and instead, decided to stay behind and enjoy the luxuries of his palace. Traditionally, the king would lead his troops into battle. David opted to remain at home and found himself with too much time on his hands and nothing to do.

One day, David arose from an afternoon nap and decided to walk out on the rooftop of his palace. Because of the way that homes in this area were designed, it was possible for someone to look in the courtyard of another's home at any given moment. David's palace was positioned above the house of Bathsheba, so, while on his rooftop, he was able to look down and see Bathsheba bathing her beautiful body. This was more than just a glance—David began to gaze and lust after this woman, who was the wife of one his elite officers, Uriah the Hittite. David's libido was raging. Though he was aware of Bathsheba's marital staus, it did not matter, he saw something he wanted, no matter what the risk.

Don't Blame Bathsheba

So David sent for Bathsheba to come to his chamber, and because of his kingship status she could not refuse, so she went. Many scholars have tried to flip this incident to make Bathsheba out as the aggressor, but there are at least four reasons why we should not blame Bathsheba for this sexual encounter.

1. David should have been at war. Perhaps Bathsheba didn't even know David was home, and therefore, did not take the necessary precautions to guard herself.

2. Even if Bathsheba knew David was home, she chose to take her bath during the time when David should have been asleep. In the eastern cultures, the king was known to take a nap right at midday. Knowing this, perhaps Bathsheba thought David was asleep when in all actuality he was checking her out.

3. David pursued Bathsheba, not the other way around. She was merely washing her body as she would do daily. The only thing different on this day as opposed to any other was that David was looking.

4. The king was powerful, and Bathsheba, as an ordinary citizen, had no way to refuse the king. Had she chosen to refuse, it could have meant trouble for her and her husband. So to keep the peace, she consented and went to the palace.

Bathsheba entered into David's chamber, and David had his way with her. Apparently the two only spent one night together, however this one night of sex eventually led to a mess that would affect more than just the two sexual partners. Bathsheba ended up pregnant.

David sought to cover up his sin of adultery by bringing Uriah, Bathsheba's husband, home from the war, in hopes that he would make love to his wife and then take credit for the pregnancy. Because of Uriah's loyalty to David and because of the fact that a soldier was not supposed to engage in sex in the middle of a war, Uriah refrained from sleeping with his wife. This left David with only his back-up plan now—he must have Uriah killed. David arranged to have Uriah killed in the heat of battle, making it look like another wartime casualty. David then took Bathsheba to be his wife, looking like a hero for taking in the widow. The baby conceived of David and Bathsheba's union is born, and then shortly after birth, dies.

There are many lessons we can glean from this particular season of David's life that give us warning about the dangers of wrong sexual relationships.

Rooftop Sex

I am one who believes in paying attention to symbolism. I don't belive it is a coincidence that David is tempted while lifted high upon the roof of his palace. This understanding is critical if we are seeking to discern when we are most vulnerable to sexual influence. It is important that you learn how to recognize the sexual vulnerabilities that spring up when you are on the rooftop of your life.

The rooftop experiences of life are really times of celebration, times of relief, times of wanting to be free and let go. It is at these moments that you must be keenly aware of what makes you weak and vulnerable, because while you are enjoying the sweetness of success on the rooftop, it is then that you may be most tempted to enhance your celebration with sex.

Rooftop sex occurs when you find yourself becoming sexually aroused because of your status, position, or success at that moment. Who doesn't want to be in somebody's arms after receiving a promotion at work, after being awarded Man of the Year by the company, or after discovering that you aced that test you've studied so hard for? Who wants to celebrate by themselves when they are drafted to their favorite team or when they just won the election or preached a great sermon?

All of these are rooftop moments that can lead to rooftop sex, if you do not build the discipline to properly handle yourself in these situations.

The enemy doesn't just come after you when you are weak—he will also try to catch you in the sexual trap when you are at the top of your career, the pinnacle of your ministry, when you become what is happening around town, when you start rising in influence. Guard against his schemes because there is a war going on, not like the war that Israel was fighting in David's day, but a war for your emotions, stability, purity and your destiny.

> *The enemy doesn't just come after you when you are weak.*

There is an old adage that says, "It is lonely at the top." It has been stated that people who have an addiction to sex are actually motivated by loneliness. "Most people caught in the world of sexual promiscuity of addiction feel a deep, heavy loneliness. Their loneliness is caused by the sexual addiction, but in too many cases the person believes that the sexual addiction is the answer to loneliness."[1] I once had a conversation with a woman who confessed to me that she was a stripper and often engaged in causual sex. After getting past the fact that she was so open about sharing this with me, I began to look beyond her fault to see her need. While she talked to me with dark shades on her eyes, I listened to her story. I noticed that she came up with story after story about broken relationships that left her feeling lonely and rejected. When I asked the woman to remove her glasses, I saw in her eyes a little girl who was looking for validation. So I validated her, and began to speak to her about the future that God had in store for her, about how her destiny was much better than her reality. She listened and began to cry, and then she said to me, "Everybody needs somebody, and I just chose a career where the somebody doesn't have to stay with me."

Instead of pursuing a sexual relationship God's way, allowing the man God had prepared for her to be sent by Him, this woman chose the poor substitute of "any man." She chose to form sexual relationships on her terms, getting rid of the person before they got rid of her. In the same way, David decided to pursue a sexual relationship his way, and left a wave of hurt, pain and agony in his wake.

The Real Sex Toys

One of the largest profit sharing industries today is in the sale of sex toys. Sex toys are sold in stores, at private parties, on the Internet, and some are even homemade. A sex toy is used during the sexual act to enhance pleasure, to make the act more gratifying, or they can serve as a substitute for human interaction. But I contend that these objects are not the only sex toys—a person who is seen as an object, whose feelings are not respected, who is viewed only as a means for the sexual gratification of another—in my opinion, that person could be referred to as a human sex toy.

David did not love Bathsheba when he first had sex with her, this was a one-night stand. The moment was just an occasion for David to spill his semen, which ultimately gave him physical gratification. This is not God's plan for sex. Such activity devalues sex and the purpose God intended for it.

> *Such activity devalues sex and the purpose God intended for it.*

Consider how beautiful and romantic sex God's way can be. In Song of Solomon 2:1-7, it is recorded,

I am the rose of Sharon, and the lily of the valleys. Like a lily among thorns, so is my love among the daughters. Like an apple tree among the trees of the wood, so is my beloved among the sons. I sat down in his shade with great delight, and his fruit was sweet to my taste. He brought me to the banqueting house, and his banner over me was love. Sustain me with cakes of raisins, refresh me with apples, for I am lovesick. His left hand is under my head, and his right hand embraces me. I charge you, O daughters of Jerusalem, by the gazelles or by the does of the field, Do not stir up nor awake love, until it pleases (NKJV).

Here is an image of what God desires for sexual love to be like. In later chapters in the Song of Solomon, apparently the women in the king's court were trying to convince the Shulamite woman that she should abandon her first love. We do not know if he had been neglecting her or if he had a history of being with other women, for whatever reason, all we know is that her girlfriends were trying to talk her out of her relationship with her first love. But it is difficult for her to leave because in her mind all she can think of is how he makes her feel loved, and romantically she begins to recall those moments.

The *Old Testament Series Commentary* describes it this way:

The Shulamite here goes back in thought to the scenes of her home-life, and the sweet days of first love. She is longingly looking for the arrival of her shepherd lover. At last she hears him. Excitement mounts: "Behold! he comes!" at least in her imagination. He is as anxious to be with her, as she is to be with him. He comes "leaping upon the mountains, skipping upon the hills."

The maiden describes her beloved as "a roe or a young hart." Both animals are shy. She is within the house when the beloved arrives. "Behold, he stands behind our wall, he looks in at the windows, he shows himself through the lattice." He stands behind the wall outside the house. He playfully looks through the windows, now through one and now through another, seeking her with his longing eyes. At last the shepherd speaks: "My beloved spoke, and said unto me, Rise up, my love, my fair one and come away."

The two of them began to take a walk, it is clear that the Shulamite woman stands out among all of the other ladies in the palace. In this discourse, the Shualamite woman begans to recite in her mind the moments that he made her feel loved. He said words like this to her, "As the apple tree among the trees of the wood so is my beloved among the sons." The apple tree is noted for the fragrance of its blossom and the sweetness of its fruit. "Trees of the wood" would be those which are wild, their fruit sour and rough. Many of the wild trees had neither flower nor fruit. Solomon is telling her that he is the man for her, and he stands out like an apple tree among fruitless trees.[2]

Thoughts of delight send the maiden into a virtual trance. She loses sense of her surroundings and imagines herself with her lover again in places the young lovers frequented in the past. She declares that his banner of love is over her. "Banner" is a military term, but in this context, it suggests that he is protecting her, and has her covered. This banner also serves notice to other men that this maiden is off limits. This banner of love was like her diamond engagement ring. "These thoughts of her beloved make the Shulamite physically weak. She is overcome by her emotion; she is in a state of ecstasy...... She has been made 'sick' of love, i.e., she is desperately love sick."[3]

In her ecstasy, the maiden recalls the moment when they were about to make love. She said, *His left hand is under my head, and his right hand embraces me* (Song of Solomon 2:6). The word *embrace* brings to mind the image of strong arms encircling about her. By her words, we know she enjoyed the moment of being in her lover's strong arms. Her recall of this moment is particularly significant because she is in need of her lover's strength at this time when her "girlfriends" are trying to talk her into throwing away her love for him.

God is no stranger to eroticism and sensual expression.

Read through the book of Song of Solomon and you will see that God is no stranger to eroticism and sensual expression. Sex can be a tremendous expression of love when it is practiced according to the will and plan of God. It is clear that the woman speaking in the Song of Solomon was a priority to her lover, and he certainly had fully committed himself to her. They had formed a union. This is the type of situation in which God desires for sexual relations to be expressed. Sex and sexual partners should not be things we treat like a toy. In the same way, you must be determined that you are not going to be treated like a toy, providing entertainment for people who have nothing better to do with their lives but play sexual games with you.

The real sex toys are not inanimate objects that are used for sexual gratification, but the real sex toys are people who allow their bodies to be used for sex simply for pleasure, with no real meaning attached to it as God destined. If you are not certain if you are currently being used as a sex toy or if you would like to prevent falling into this trap in the future, here are a few telltale signs to look for:

1. If your quality time with your mate is only spent in the bed, you are being used as a sex toy.

2. If there is no accountablility in the relationship, and if the only time you matter is when it is time for sexual pleasure, you are being used as a sex toy.

3. If the only thing mentioned about your attributes is your performance in bed—never anything about your mind, spirit, personality, your goals and desires for greatness— you are being used as a sex toy.

4. If the only intimate calls you get are at night when the world has shut down, and there is nothing else to do but have sex, you are being used as a sex toy. This is commonly referred to as a "booty call."

5. If your definition of a quality relationship centers around sex and you are, even now, settling for this reality in the relationship, you have convinced yourself that you are nothing but a sex toy.

6. If you consistently feel a sense of emptiness, loneliness, or disconnection from God after the act of sex, take these as warning signs from God, trying to tell you to stop being used as a sex toy. This was not His design for sex and certainly not His plan for your life.

Bathsheba was David's sex toy. At the time he called her to his chambers, he didn't have any long range plans for her, he was just a king who wanted what he wanted. This is the wrong kind of sexual relationship and any time you step outside of God's plans, it is important to remember that there are consequences which can affect both you and others. Remember what happened in this saga between David and Bathsheba.

Out of Order Sex Can Cause Death

The Word is clear when it says, *The wages of sin is death; but the gift of God is eternal life through Jesus Christ our Lord* (Romans 6:23). A wage is something that is earned. The sin David committed earned him much strife and grief. In the Hebrew languages there are three meanings for the word sin. The first word is *chatta'ah (sin)*, which means to miss the mark, to fall short of a projected goal or plan. The next word is *pesha* (transgression) which means a conscious, calculated, intentional dismissal of divine standard. *Avon* (iniquity) is a twisting of the standard, to make the standard conducive for personal gain.[4] In the actions of David described in 2 Samuel 11, we see all three forms of sin surfacing.

After their one-night stand, Bathsheba ends up pregnant. This untimely and unexpected pregnancy put into motion a cycle of bad decisions. Most of the time it is not the mistakes that we make in life that destroy us, but it is the things we do to cover up the mistake that lead to our downfall. When David discovered that Bathsheba was pregnant, he arranged for her husband, Uriah, to be killed in battle. But this is only the first death that will result from David's sin. The second death took place when the baby Bathsheba conceived with David also died. David's out of order sexual choices led to two physical deaths, but we will see that there were also spiritual deaths associated with the sin of David as well.

Death from Out of Order Sex

Sex that is practiced out of order will cause something to die. While the death may not always be the physical death of a child or a spouse, as was the case with David and Bathsheba, know that out of order sex can kill your destined relationship with God, it can kill your future, your trust, and your chance to do life God's way.

Sex that is practiced out of order will cause something to die.

There are many people who are living with the guilt of giving up their virginity to someone who did not respect them, never intended to love them, and certainly never intended to marry them. Living with guilt may not always lead to physical death, though it certainly has in some instances, but it will always leave you feeling less alive. Out of order sex can lead to the destruction of a relationship that really could have been good for the rest of your life.

Out of order sex can lead to a myriad of physical problems including herpes, syphilis, HIV/AIDS, chlamydia and other sexually translated diseases. When the enemy really wants to destroy you with out of order sex, he will tempt you to take more and more risks as you engage in sexual activities. The destructive spirit of Satan could lead you to a place where sex with the opposite gender is not enough, now you desire to experiment with same-sex partners or engage in orgies with multiple partners, always in a quest to fill the void within. This is absolutely what it means to live a life of spiritual death due to out of order sex.

Cheating on Your Lover

One of the things that the Tiger Woods saga reminded the world, is that cheating still happens today in all kinds of relationships. If you are in a committed relationship, cheating can bring death. Maybe not physical death, but death of possibilities.

Out of order sex has caused many marriages and relationships to be destroyed. There was once a couple in my church who had a beautiful marriage, lovely children, and both partners projected a sense that everything was well with their lives. However, the wife's need for more validation led her to enter into conversation with another man on the Internet. The Internet chats led to dinner, dinner led to a car ride, the car ride led to a hotel room, and the hotel room led to the destruction of the marriage. Sadly, this couple is no longer married and they are living in two different states.

The question that you must ask yourself when you are considering putting so much on the line is this, *Is it worth it?* Is ten minutes of erotic and exciting thrill worth your established reputation among family and friends? Is it worth your career or ministry accomplishments? Is it worth risking the reputation you have worked so hard to establish of being a person of character and integrity? Is it worth it? Tiger Woods lost a lot, and most of what he lost he may never be able to recover. For years, he worked to build an image of class and integrity. His sexual decisions put all of that in jeopardy. Yes, he is playing golf again, but you can believe that he has lost sleep over what he has done to his wife, children, family, friends and supporters. Is it worth it?

This is another form of death, and it is happening even in the church. Out of order sex can make a praise and worship leader lose the fire for leading worship. It can make a preacher hang his head on Sunday morning when he comes to the portion of the Word dealing with sexual purity. Out of order sex will make it necessary for a deacon to have to apologize before the open congregation about his unworthiness to serve. It will cause a youth worker to have to step down from serving as a youth leader in the church. Out of order sex will cause one to weep at the altar Sunday after Sunday, week after week. Out of order sex will lead to a church secretary having a secret abortion without her husband knowing about it, while the business director of the church is forced to pay for it out of an account that his wife doesn't have access to. Out of order sex can lead to destruction of character and will hinder the work of the kingdom of God.

In this affair involving David and Bathsheba, I am convinced that Bathsheba was more a victim than a willing participant. But it is apparent that David committed all three forms of sin that we mentioned earlier in this chapter. David clearly missed the mark (*hata*) when he used his position of authority as an instrument for sexual aggression, in compelling Bathsheba to have sex with him. He committed the sin of transgression (*pesa*) when he consciously devised a plan to cover up the pregancy of Bathsheba, and then when that plan failed, to have Bathsheba's husband murdered. He committed the sin of iniquity (*awon*) when he married another man's wife to eradicate his own guilt while attempting to increase his standing in the eyes of others. David did all of this in the context of this wrong sexual relationship.

How Do You Make a Wrong Sexual Relationship Right?

LISTEN TO NATHAN

I would like to call 2 Samuel 11, the 11th Chapter of David's life. In this chapter, David committed acts that would ultimately bring judgment upon him. Now, in the 12th chapter of 2 Samuel, we find where the judgment is executed. Never forget that for every action there is a consequence. We read in 2 Samuel 12 that God spoke to a prophet named Nathan, and it is Nathan who came to David and began to speak a parable to him about a poor man and a rich man. (See 2 Samuel 12:1-6.) At the end of the telling, the point of the parable is driven home to David by these simple words from Nathan: *You're the man!* (2 Samuel 12:7 MSG). Nathan continues with the message from God:

> *And here's what GOD, the God of Israel, has to say to you: I made you king over Israel. I freed you from the fist of Saul. I gave you your master's daughter and other wives to*

For every action there is a consequence.

have and to hold. I gave you both Israel and Judah. And if that hadn't been enough, I'd have gladly thrown in much more. So why have you treated the word of GOD with brazen contempt, doing this great evil? You murdered Uriah the Hittite, then took his wife as your wife. Worse, you killed him with an Ammonite sword! And now, because you treated God with such contempt and took Uriah the Hittite's wife as your wife, killing and murder will continually plague your family. This is GOD speaking, remember! I'll make trouble for you out of your own family. I'll take your wives from right out in front of you. I'll give them to some neighbor, and he'll go to bed with them openly. You did your deed in secret; I'm doing mine with the whole country watching!" Then David confessed to Nathan, "I've sinned against GOD." Nathan pronounced, "Yes, but that's not the last word. GOD forgives your sin. You won't die for it. But because of your blasphemous behavior, the son born to you will die."

(2 Samuel 12:7-14 MSG)

Nathan gives David a word of judgment, speaking to him nothing but truth and shedding light on the mess that he has made. David could have refuted Nathan, but instead he humbles himself and receives the words of Nathan as God lets David know he was wrong.

The Nathan in You

God has given a Nathan to all of us—a prophet, a voice, a friend inside of all of

> *God has given a Nathan to all of us.*

us that will let us know when we are wrong and out of order. Many times we try to justify ourselves in our minds, saying that since the wrong we have been doing has not been called out by our preacher, parents, parishioners, or our friends, therefore, what we are doing must not really be that wrong. But in the same way that God spoke to Nathan, He will speak to the Nathan in your spirit, to let you know that you are engaging in behavior that's going to ultimately destroy you. More importantly, He will show you that what you are doing continues to hurt God. The Nathan in your spirit will tell you, "You are better than this, you deserve more than what you are settling for, the feeling of whoredom does not fit with your destiny." Listen to the Nathan in your spirit, listen to God's voice, because that voice is right and true.

Listening to the Nathan in your spirit is hard, because it means that there are some things that you are going to have leave and let go of. There are some pleasures that you are going to have to forsake and there are some people you are going to have to take out of your cell phone, take off your e-mail list, not to mention getting your stuff out of their bed.

While there is a Nathan in your spirit, it is also important to learn to listen to the Nathans God will send into your path. The Nathan in your path sometimes shows up in conversations with people who have been there and done that. Sometimes Nathans can be heard from pulpits, on the porch of a grandmother's house, or even from the mouth of an innocent child who mentions a word that will bring tears to your eyes about your reality. Whatever "Nathan" God chooses to use to get to you, listen, because listening is the first step down the road to make a wrong sexual relationship right.

Learn to Repent

Then David confessed to Nathan, "I've sinned against God."

(2 Samuel 12:13 MSG)

Repentance is the most critical part of making a wrong sexual relationship right. Once you acknowledge the voice of Nathan inside of you or in your path, you have to repent. Repenting involves acknowledging where you have violated God's law, but more than that, repenting involves surrendering to God's plan and turning away from your sin. Repentance is powerful because it allows you to be spiritually naked before God. There is nothing hidden, everything is revealed and there are no longer secrets of which to be ashamed. Repentance is asking God to forgive you for not trusting in Him to fill your void when you looked to the flesh to satisfy your need. Repentance is not only apologizing to God, but it is also means you apologize to yourself. Forgive yourself, take the experiences and learn from them, make better choices as you start your life over again.

Get Back on Duty

Getting back on duty simply means that after everything is said and done, after the bad choices have been made, after you've heard Nathan and have repented for your wrong doings, it is time for you to get back on track to pursue the destiny that God has promised to you.

After all of this drama with Bathsheba, in 2 Samuel 12:26-30, David received a word from Joab, who was at war with the Ammorites, requesting David's help to fight this war. David gathered his troops, went out to battle, and won the war. This is key when you are trying to recover from serious sexual sins, because once you realize that you have been in a wrong sexual relationship, now that you are taking corrective steps to fix it, you have to get back to the assignment God has given you in life. Your assignment is waiting on you, and while others may have placed judgment on you, your assignment will never judge you. Regardless of the bad decisions you have made in the past concerning your sexual life, God still has work for you to do.

God still has work for you to do.

Perhaps this is why John Thompson declared, "Travel light! Be rid of all excess baggage, for at times the way may be rocky and difficult, up steep slopes, and around dangerous precipices. Travel light! So do not carry excess baggage of guilt, of regrets from the past, of unforgiven sin. Hear the assurance of God's own Word, As far as the East is from the West, so far have I removed your sins from you. Glory be to God!"[5]

How to Date After Listening to Nathan, Repenting, and Getting Back on Duty

Dr. Willie Richardson, in his book, *Reclaiming the Urban Family*, reveals a profound paradigm for establishing a godly relationship. In his book, he records the steps that a single person should take when seeking to establish a relationship with someone special in their life: Casual Friendships, Close Friends, Intimate Friends, Engagement, and Marriage.[6]

FIRST STEP—CASUAL FRIENDSHIPS

Richardson says that at this stage, you are just meeting the person and learning as much as you can about them. At this level, nothing in the relationship is real deep, you are just meeting, talking, and getting to know one another. There is still the option for you or them to date others, and this should be understood by both. "Don't be mislead when someone who is interested in you tells you, 'God laid you on my heart,' or 'God promised you to me.' Just remember, God is intelligent enough to tell you Himself."[7] At this level there is no patting and no kissing, handshakes will do just fine.

SECOND STEP—CLOSE FRIENDS

As the friendship grows stronger and both of you approach a point where you know one another better, light expectations begin to set in. At this level, dates are more frequent, however it is still understood that the two of you may be dating others. At this level, there is a deeper conversation that takes place concerning goals and objectives, spiritual insight, political ideals, social opinions, and what it means to each of you to be in a committed relationship. At this level, the two of you may pray together, read scripture together, and just simply make yourselves available for one another to "vent" and share general ideas. At this level, there is still no patting and no kissing, handshakes are still just fine.

Third Step—Intimate Friendship

After about 12 months of developing the relationship, you reach the next level when you have both decided to date each other exclusively. The terms of the relationship have shifted from just being casual friends, to where both of you feel called to something more serious. "There should be a commitment to invest at least 12 months at this level and this could be an exception depending on the relationship. The two people must be very inquisitive; you cannot learn too much about each other. This is precisely the reason that some single people want a quick courtship; they are afraid that something will be discovered that they want to hide."[8]

At this stage, you can do fun, intimate things like read the Bible and discuss scripture while sitting in front of the fireplace. Cook a meal together while sharing stories about God and the miracles He has performed in your lives. If you are faced with great temptation, you can always change the atmosphere by playing gospel music in the background. It is hard to be thinking illicit things when "Blessed Assurance, Jesus Is Mine" is playing in the background.

At this level you can be yourself, as you are checking the potential of this person as a husband or wife. At this stage, you are looking to see how well they keep house, their habit of handling business, and determine if this person would be a good fit for you for the rest of your life. At this level there may be some kissing involved, but it is important to know how much you can bear without being tempted to cross the line into inappropriate behavior. Take your time at this level to be certain that you are ready for the next level of relationship.

Fourth Step—Engagement

You have now reached the level of the relationship where it is time to get engaged. The engagement ring is a symbol of commitment to marry, so obviously at this stage, interaction with each other will be much more substantive. The conversation is different at this level, and the first thing you must confirm is the level of commitment to a lifelong relationship. If you are not serious about giving up "you", for "y'all" then there is no point entering this stage of the relationship. "The focus in the relationship turns from getting to know one another better to a wedding day."[9] At this level there should be movement toward discarding the "single mentality." In other words, there is no talk about "I, mine, and me," there is more of a mindset of being a team. You should plan to engage in at least six months of marital counseling where there should be discussion about family, how many children you desire to have, what will be the rules for in-laws, how you are going to manage financial obligations, child disciplinary forms, and the role of the husband and the wife as it pertains to the good of the relationship.

FIFTH STEP—MARRIAGE

It is important that before you enter into this covenant agreement that you understand the words *love* and *sacrifice*. Marriage according to God's plan, can be a beautiful means for ministry. In other words, your marriage must be seen as a ministry. It is important that the two of you understand that God is uniting you to serve and be a blessing to one another and to the kingdom of God. Every marriage has its trials and its temptations, but you have already overcome with the help of God. In marriage, you have to be determined to remain committed and faithful, realizing that it is always a good thing to sacrifice for the one that you have professed before God and others that you love. And yes, at this level, you can have all the sex you want!

Sexual Relationship Reflection Questions

1. Do you have a healthy understanding of the intention that God has for sex?

2. Do you or does anyone in your family have a sexual addiction according to the definition given in this chapter?

3. There is a section in this chapter that mentions "rooftop sex." Why do you think sex becomes more tempting once we reach a level of achievement or success?

4. What principles or disciplines must be in place for Christians to guard themselves against out of control sexual behaviors?

5. Have you or has anyone you know ever been used as a sex toy according to the definition given in this chapter? What toll has that taken on their self-esteem? On their walk with Christ?

6. Dr. Willie Richardson's steps for dating are discussed in this chapter. What are some of the benfits of following the dating plan that is suggested?

CHAPTER 9

❧

MAKING A WRONG
Parent-Child Relationship Right

The king was stunned. Heartbroken, he went up to the
room over the gate and wept. As he wept he cried out,
   O my son Absalom, my dear, dear son Absalom!
   Why not me rather than you, my death and not yours,
   O Absalom, my dear, dear son!

2 Samuel 18:33 MSG

Recently the comedian and actress Mo'Nique won her
very first Golden Globe award for best actress for her role in
the movie *Precious*. This movie is centered around an obese,
illiterate, 16-year-old girl named Claireece "Precious" Jones,
who lives in the ghetto of Harlem. Her dysfunctional mother,
Mary, (played by Mo'Nique) had been impregnated twice by
her father, and lived her life in a vacuum of damaging abuse.
When Precious gets pregnant for the second time, she is sus-
pended from school and ends up in an alternative school.
Because of the intervention of many caring people, Precious

then begins to put her life together by slowly dealing with her painful reality.

The character played by Mo'Nique shed many tears on screen during the movie. The tears she shed on the screen were mirrors of the tears Mo'Nique has cried in real life. Mo'Nique has a history of molestation and sexual abuse herself. Recently, Mo'Nique's brother confessed to Oprah Winfrey that he molested Mo'Nique when he was 12 and she was 7, by bribing her with candy to allow him to touch her and to have sex with her. While Mo'Nique is funny on stage, in reality she has lived a very painful private life. Sadly, this is not just a modern problem. This kind of family dysfunction is similar to a reality experienced by David within his own family.

The events described in 2 Samuel 13 through 15 take place just as David is recovering from the guilt of having an affair with Bathsheba and the judgment that came as a result of that wrong sexual relationship. Just when David thought that he had experienced as much as he could bear, his daughter Tamar is raped by her half brother, Amnon, David's eldest son.

Earlier in this book, I talked about the reality of generational curses. If ever there was an example of a generational curse, this is one. An out of control sexual spirit can be manifested in different ways without warning. This spirit manifested itself through David in the way that he took advantage of somebody else's wife. Now that same out of control sexual spirit is causing David's eldest son, Amnon, to take advantage of his half-sister. A demonic spirit does not know boundaries, and its sole purpose is to wreak havoc while satisfying its own need.

How did David's precious daughter come to be raped by her brother? How could this have happened? It all began when David's son Amnon allowed himself to develop unnatural feelings for his own sister, Tamar. Amnon, with the help of his unscrupulous friend Jonadab, devised a scheme to get his sister into his bedroom by acting like he was sick, but in the end, this scheme would serve to make Tamar sick. (2 Samuel 13:1-5.)

When Tamar came in the room with a bowl of soup, Amnon grabbed her and snatched her into the bed. Imagine the scene as described in 2 Samuel 13:9-14: while Tamar is kicking and fighting and screaming, Amnon puts his hand over her mouth and penetrates this virgin girl, caring nothing about the pain and agony that she is feeling. There is not much record of Tamar's response to this rape, outside of what we read in 2 Samuel 13:18-20. We know that Tamar lived out her days in her brother Absalom's house, bitter and desolate.

Though we don't have record of Tamar's exact thoughts, I believe her experience must have been like that of German girl, Gabi Köpp, who has written a book about her rape experience entitled, *Warum war ich bloss ein Mädchen?* (*Why Did I Have to Be a Girl?*)[1] The book was an unprecedented document, in that it was the first book written voluntarily by a woman who was raped. Köpp was raped in the final months of World War II by soldiers who had been charged with protecting her. She recalls the experience as a "place of horror" and a "door to hell."

While it was a terrible thing for this German woman to be raped by soldiers who should have been protecting her, without comparing the pain and shame, I would dare to say that Tamar's situation was even worse. Tamar was raped by her brother, her blood, someone she trusted with her well being. It was this rape that ushered in another wave of drama for David and his family. David discovers that Amnon has raped his daughter, Tamar, and as if that was not bad enough, now another son, Absalom, is out to kill Amnon.

Absalom eventually does succeed in killing his half-brother, Amnon, to avenge the violation of Tamar. (2 Samuel 13:23-29.) In fear of David's anger at the killing of Amnon, Absalom flees the country. David finds himself faced with two choices—he could have had Absalom hunted down and executed for the murder, or he could have tried to restore him through encouraging confession and offering forgiveness. Sadly, David took neither course. He eventually did allow Absalom to return home, but he refused to see Absalom for a time and when he did eventually see him face to face, the meeting was distant as an air of unforgiveness permeated the hall. (2 Samuel 14:21-33.)

The longer Absalom's sin remained not dealt with, the longer it festered until eventually, the country split. Absalom convinced a number of people to follow him rather than

David, which further alienated father from son. Absalom went so far as to have himself crowned king to dethrone his father, which forced David to flee from the capital to save his life. (2 Samuel 15:10-14.) How deeply it must have cut David to see people who once supported him, now supporting a revolt against him, led by his own son.

None of this should have taken David by surprise. The prophet, Nathan, told David in 2 Samuel 12:11-12, *Thus saith the LORD, Behold, I will raise up evil against thee out of thine own house, and I will take thy wives before thine eyes, and give them unto thy neighbour, and he shall lie with thy wives in the sight of this sun. For thou didst it secretly: but I will do this thing before all Israel, and before the sun.*

The rest of the story is no better than the first. Though David does return to the throne, in the process, he loses another son. Though David had given direct orders not to lay a hand on Absalom, in the heat of battle, Absalom does, indeed, lose his life. The story ends with David crying out in agony and weeping over both of his lost sons, and the rape of his daughter. (2 Samuel 18.)

While there are many issues that we could focus in on from this story such as rape, incest, sibling rivalry, murder, and the results of immoral behavior, the one issue that I want to fully examine here concerns this very dysfunctional, broken parent/child relationship between David and Absalom. Psychologist Sigmond Freud devised a theory he called the "Oedipus Complex." The Oedipus complex derived its name from the Greek mythological story of Oedipus, who had a desire to have his mother all to himself. In order to accomplish this, he determined to kill his father, who was the king, and then claim his mother as his wife. Freud used this theory, in part, to describe the psychological tension between a father and a son. In the case of David and Absalom, however, the female source of tension is not a wife, but it is Tamar, the daughter of David and the sister of Absalom.

The situation between Absalom and David begs the question, what do you do when there is a strain between a parent and a child? What do you do when the child you raised projects so much envy and dislike toward you, that it is obvious that in their heart, they desire you to be out of their lives? How do you cope, when your own child rises to make certain that you are destroyed, or when your parent wishes that your ultimate destiny is failure? Strained parent / child relationships are a common reality and they are more prevalent now than ever before. In light of this fact, the question that we need to raise is how do you make this wrong relationship right?

The behavior you model is being observed by very impressionable eyes, minds, and hearts.

As a Parent, Model a Right Example

It is important, if you are a parent or a guardian of a child, that you understand how much of an impact you have on the shaping of your child. The behavior you model is being observed by very impressionable eyes, minds, and hearts. David had modeling issues. The example he set of being a father reflected his lack of discipline and respect. In the account we considered in this chapter, we see that the behavior David modeled is now coming forth from his sons, who would ultimately lose their lives as a result of their decisions.

There is an old adage that says, "Don't do as I do, but do as I say." While that might be great wishful thinking, it is not realistic. Children often do as we do. Because of this, you must make it a priority to model positive actions in front of your children. Take inventory of your actions—do you make it a habit to curse, drink, smoke, practice recreational drug use, practice forms of abuse, steal or even disrepect God and the church in front of your children?

I had a former church member who was very critical towards the church. In her opinion, the church could not do anything right, and in her mind, nobody in the church was right. This was the case until her daughter got hooked on drugs. When that happened, she told her daughter she needed to go to church and pray. The daughter's response was "Why should I go to church? For years, you told me it was on its way to hell." Parents, be careful what you model and say about the church in front of your child, because one day the church may be all that you have to get your child out of hell.

Recently I had a conversation with a woman who shared with me about a strained relationship that she had with her son. While this woman, in the past, had always presented herself as a strong, happy, and family-oriented woman, on this day I saw the burden on her brow. She began to tell me that her 14-year-old son had developed a strong hate for her. She stated that, upon her telling him to clean up his room and be more responsible about doing his household chores, he became irate and threatened to hit her while at the same time yelling, "I wish you were dead!" While I was shocked to hear of this kind of rage coming from her son, before I knew it, I asked the question, "Who is your son modeling in the home?" She responded by saying, "My husband and his father." She began to share with me how the father moves in and out of rages, his temper causing him to curse and throw things at her. Adding to the problem, he never takes a moment to discipline the children when they act as he does. This is an example of a child modeling the negative behavior of a parent.

Before we get too discouraged, I want to point out that not all modeling is negative. Children can model positive behavior as well. Reinforce your expectations for positive behavior in your children with your own positive behavior. Keep in mind that there will be other influences at school, on television, on the Internet, and in their social setting that may counteract your positive influence and encourage negative behavior, but you, as the parent, have the chance to make the greatest impact because your relationship will last the longest. As long as you and your child are alive, you will have opportunity to deliberately model good behavior.

As a Parent, Be Firm About Your Standard

In this post-modern era, one of the difficulties that parents face is knowing where to draw the line between being a parent and being a friend. As a parent, it is good if you can be friendly, but you are not your child's friend, you are their parent. One of the things that I noticed about David is that he never allowed his mistakes to compromise the standard that he had for his children. Yes, David did model some poor behavior, but he still maintained a high level of expectation for his children. This fact becomes clear when David becomes furious with Absalom after Amnon is killed. Though Absalom may have believed he had reason to kill his brother Amnon because of what he had done to Tamar, David still maintained that it was not right for brother to kill brother.

You are not your child's friend, you are their parent.

While I pray that you never have to arbitrate a fight like this one between Absalom and Amnon, setting a standard for your child is still your duty as a parent. What is your expectation of them as it pertains to school work? Do your children know where you stand on the issues of pre-marital sex or smoking? Do they understand how important you feel it is that they speak the truth and do they know the consequences they will face should they choose not to? Does your child know how you really feel about them walking around in tight clothes, with spiked hair, tattoos in sensual places, or with their belly rings showing while walking in the mall? Do they know that you need to know who they are dating or spending time with? If you do not know for certain that your children know these things, Parent, regardless of how much of a protest your child may put up, it is your job to speak truth and set the standard. If they say to you, "You can't tell me what to do, because of what you have done," please make it clear to them that it is not about what you have done, it is about what they are expected to do. And what is expected is that your rules are going to be followed, especially as long as you are the one who is paying the bills!

Setting a standard is the key for the success of the home. The story has been told of the mother who knew her teenage son was involved in illegal activities. This mother noticed her son hanging around unfavorable friends, but she remained silent as he began to buy expensive jewelry. She turned her head when he flashed all the money he had. But she drew the line when she discovered the bloody clothes and the gun in his pocket. She turned her only son into the police. When the officers asked her what made her call them, she simply said, "It is a lot easier for me to visit him in prison every week, than for me to visit him once at his grave."[2]

Being a parent is not easy, it requires making some hard decisions, however, it is better to make hard decisions now than to let your child continue going astray and deal with the consequences later. When you make these standards non-negotiable, your child may get mad, but you would rather have them angry for a time than have them miss their destiny having engaged in wrong relationships.

Helpful Hints for Parents
Seeking to Get Along with Their Children

- Learn how to model your parenting skills after biblical instruction, especially in the areas of love and sacrifice.

- Reflect on your relationship with your parents. Be aware of the things that you enjoyed about their parenting, and the things that were not so positive for you. Try to emulate those things that were effective, and try not to repeat those things that were hurtful to you.

- It is important for you to pay attention to your children, and learn to embrace their individualism. If you have more than one child, do not get caught up in comparing one with the other, and by all means, do not show favoritism. Though your love may not be equal, it should be equitable.

- Be mindful of discussing grown up issues with children. For the sake of your children, never voice ill opinions of your spouse in front of them. You must forsake your right to voice complaints about your marital relationship in front of the children.

Children, Don't Undo the Work

Absalom sought to undo the work of his father by seeking to split the kingom his father had unified by his many efforts. Absalom was selfish, cynical, narcissistic, opportunistic, and arrogant. All of these traits have the potential of bringing any family dynasty down.

It is important that children understand the necessity of not competing with their parents. It is all for the good of the same family. Undoing the good work of your parents cannot be justified under the guise of "making the situation they left you better." If you have inherited the family business, then build upon it and take it from regional to global. If you have inherited family property, by all means pay taxes on it, improve the property and don't let it go into foreclosure. If you have been given a good name that people honor and respect, you must protect that name with integrity and character.

Children, Know Your Place

Children need to understand that they are a direct reflection of the family lineage.

Children need to understand that they are a direct reflection of the family lineage. The mere fact that you bear a last name, means that you represent a long line of people who have had that same last name. You may bear a name that you can be proud of, or it could be that you are carrying a name that you only dare voice in a whisper. Whatever the case, children carry a legacy behind them.

This is an important fact to grasp because children must know their place in relationship to their parents. Even though David made some bad decisions and those bad decisions did impact his children, Absolom and Amnon had no right to act as they did. Amnon defamed the family by raping his sister, and Absolom despised him for what he did to the point of desiring that he be dead. None of this behavior brought honor to David or the family name. In the final analysis, David was known as a man after God's own heart. The behavior of these two sons of David did not live up to the heritage they were blessed to have been given.

Here are a few things it would do children well to remember pertaining to their relationship with their parents:

- You did not have a choice in the parents you were given, but because they are your parents, respect must be extended at all times.

- If there are differences between a child and a parent, these differences can be discussed in a genuine way, but never does a child have the right to curse, verbally abuse, or storm off before the conversation is completed. Children also have the right to expect a degree of respect from the parent. The parent has the duty to set the proper tone of the conversation.

- For the child, much of what you have is because of your parents. If they are providing for you, the very least you can do is give them the respect they deserve as a return on their investment.

- Take a moment to really reflect and think about why the relationship is the way it is between you and your parents. Keep a journal of your frustration and emotions. This has proven to be most helpful in properly evaluating relationships.

- If there is a history of failures to communicate, it is always good to enlist a third party to hear both sides. After both sides have been heard, put a plan in place to rectify the divisions that exist between you.

- A child should always keep in mind while forming opinions about the effectiveness of their parent, that they may not always understand why their parents make the decisions that they make. As a child, you may not know the full story, so it is a good thing to reserve judgment until you fully learn your parent's story.

PARENT-CHILD RELATIONSHIP REFLECTION QUESTIONS

1. Do you think that David handled the drama between his children fairly or correctly?

2. Is there any experience in your own life that will allow you to relate to the position that David was placed in?

3. How do you think parenting children today is different from parenting in the past?

4. Are there any insecurities from your past that affect the way you relate to your children or to youth in general?

5. Do you believe in corporal punishment as a form of discipline? What are the pros and cons of this method of discipline? What does the Bible say about the issue and is that relevant today?

6. At what point should medication or counseling be considered to help parents relate more effectively to their children?

7. What are some practical methods that can be used to develop a solid relationship with children? Do all methods work for all children?

8. What are the benefits of parents taking time to develop a relationship with children today?

CHAPTER 10

MAKING A WRONG
Financial Relationship Right

I have worked hard to provide materials for building the Temple of the Lord—nearly 4,000 tons of gold, 40,000 tons of silver, and so much iron and bronze that it cannot be weighed. I have also gathered timber and stone for the walls, though you may need to add more.

1 Chronicles 22:14 NLT

Wealth Abiding with David

Considering all the relationships that David encountered, there is none more surprising than the one he had with finances. While many of us know David as a shepherd boy, king, warrior, and an adulterer, very seldom do we take the time to know David as a wealthy, financial industrialist.

A subtle point expressing David's relationship with wealth is established in 1 Chronicles 22:14. David had come to a point in his life where it was now time for him to pass the baton to his son Solomon. David is preparing to leave the scene, and the one last task that he wants to accomplish is to build the Temple in which Israel will worship their God, Yahweh. Similar to how God gave Moses the plans for the tabernacle (Exodus 25:40), He now gives David the plans for the Temple; however, in this situation, God denies David His goodwill to allow him to build it. To be more precise, David lost favor to build the Temple because of his guilt in shedding the blood of Uriah, and because he had so much blood on his hands from all of the wars that he led and fought. God did not find it acceptable to let a man with such a reputation for bringing death, build a place that would be intended to save lives. In His grace, however, God chose David's son Solomon, whose name in the Hebrew is taken from the word "shalom" which is interpreted as "peace," to build a house for His Name. God wanted the Temple to be built by a man of peace rather than a man of war.

Although David was not allowed to build the temple, the fact is that he possessed all of the wealth, resources, treasures, reserves, assets and materials needed to get the job done. Without a doubt, David had massive riches. Money was no object for him. In 1 Chronicles 22:13-16, David declares to Solomon, *Take charge! Don't be timid; don't hold back. Look at this—I've gone to a lot of trouble to stockpile materials for the sanctuary of GOD: a hundred thousand talents (3,775 tons) of gold, a million talents (37,750 tons) of silver, tons of bronze and iron—too much to weigh—and all this timber and stone. And you're free to add more. And workers both plentiful and prepared: stonecutters, masons, carpenters, artisans in gold and silver, bronze and iron. You're all set—get to work! And GOD-speed!* (MSG)

At the time of this writing, the cost of gold is $1,166.00 per ounce, and the cost of silver is about $18.50 per ounce. Using these figures, if we calculated the net worth of David today, he would be worth about 173 billion dollars, which would make him wealthier than Bill Gates and Warren Buffet—two of the most wealthy men in today's society. To further put the magnitude of David's wealth into perspective, *Forbes Magazine* recently stated that a Latin American man by the name of Carlos Slim Helu, who is founder of a national telecom operation, currently holds the position of being the richest person in the world; he has a net worth of nearly $54 billion.[1] Even with all of their resources, David would still have $119 billion dollars more than the richest person in the world today.

It is possible to possess a good amount of money, but at the same time, be lacking in good character as a compliment.

Finances and Character

The issue with David building the temple was never about whether or not he had enough money to do the job. On the contrary, David didn't get to build the temple because of flaws in his character. This ultimately shows that it is possible to possess a good amount of money, but at the same time, be lacking in good character as a compliment. The writer of Proverbs declares, *"A good name is more desirable than great riches; to be esteemed is better than silver or gold"* (Proverbs 22:11 NIV). You can attain riches, wealth, and prosperity in so many areas of your life, but if your character is not such that God can trust you, or if your integrity does not reflect God in your life, you most likely have a wrong relationship with finances.

When addressing matters of character and integrity, it is important for you to understand how these factors relate to your financial position. George Horace Lorimer has said, "It's good to have money and the things that money can buy, but it's good, too, to check up once in a while and make sure that you haven't lost the things that money can't buy."[2] For instance, money can't buy joy, peace, happiness, serenity, wisdom, character, integrity, and most importantly—salvation. When your relationship with money is not right, that has a way of preventing us from securing all of the aforementioned virtues.

In our culture, money has become a dominating factor in the lives of many. Money has a way of shaping our values, our beliefs, and our perceptions about ourselves and others. While this should not be, this is reality. Money can cause people to invite forms of ruin into their lives which eventually cause self destruction.

What Causes a Bad Relationship with Money

HISTORICAL IGNORANCE

Historical ignorance is one reason people form bad relationships with money. This type of ignorance stems from our introduction to how money should be valued, saved, and even spent. Most of the time, this ignorance is passed down from our parents or others who should teach us about money when we are children. As this historical ignorance is passed down from generation to generation, many people never learn how to balance a checkbook or understand how adjustable interest rates work on a credit card. These historically ignorant people never learn about stocks, bonds, investment plans, tax write offs, and they certainly never learn to follow the biblical principles of tithing.

These people seemingly have no hope of a good relationship with money because they have never been introduced to these early foundational money principles. They grow to become adults and make all kinds of mistakes with money, just as their parents did, because they were never taught how to have a right relationship with money.

You must take the initiative.

If you find yourself among the historically ignorant, there is hope for you to make a wrong relationship with money right. You must take the initiative to ask questions, seek financial advice, and be determined to tackle any areas that you feel may have you bound and oppressed in the area of finance. What did your parents teach you about money? What trends do you have that resemble their habits? How has your early orientation of money worked for you or against you?

Historical Myths that We Have Been Taught About Money

TAKEN FROM *SMART MONEY MOVES FOR AFRICAN AMERICANS* BY KELVIN BOSTON[3]

1. *Money is the root of all evil*—No, not money, but the love of money is the root for all evil.

2. *It's hard for the rich to get into heaven*—No, there are many wealthy people who will be in heaven, because they know how to distinguish having more money from having more God. Proverbs 14:23: *All hard work brings a profit, but mere talk leads only to poverty* (NIV).

3. *You can't take it with you*—No, you can't take it with you, but you can sure leave some behind. There is a generation that is coming behind you, who should one day honor you for not just living for yourself, but also living and working hard for them.

4. *My God will take care of me*—Fatalism is when you put the entire obligation on God to provide for you. Yes, God will take care of you, but you also need to take care of you. Want a job? Submit a résumé. Want more money? Get another job. Want more in life? Strive for more in life.

You need to do your part, because at Calvary, the Lord already did His.

5. *Money should not change you*—Incorrect, money has to change you. It has to change how you plan, how you invest, how you evaluate needs, how you plan for your future. Do not be afraid to let money change you, but make certain it changes you for the better.

6. *What's wrong with poor? Even Jesus was poor*—Jesus was not poor by destiny, he became poor by choice so that you can be rich. 2 Corinthians 8:9 says, *For ye know the grace of our Lord Jesus Christ, that, though he was rich, yet for your sakes he became poor, that ye through his poverty might be rich.* Get out of this mindset that poor is godly, and stop using this as an excuse, that you are being more holy by being poorer.

SPIRIT OF COMPETITION

The spirit of competition is another reason that people develop a wrong relationship with money. The spirit of competition is seen when a person seeks to live beyond their means in an effort to acquire someone else's lifestyle. There are many people today who cannot tithe, who cannot contribute to the kingdom of God because of their need to spend every dime they get in their hand. They run up credit card charges to the max, and splurge on items that they really cannot realistically afford. The spirit of competition often surfaces when people are trying to prove their worth to others with material things. I have discovered that it does not make sense to compete with the spending habits of others because, more often than not, people are not even paying attention to all that you have, and they surely will not help you pay for those things you've bought.

Marian Wright Edelman tells the story of how, years ago, she happened to be watching the inauguration of President Lyndon Johnson with a woman who was of "high class." The woman of "high class" said, "Why, there is the great civil rights leader, Fannie Lou Hamer, at the President's Ball. She doesn't even have on a long gown!"

How easy is it for us to confuse style with substance.

Edelman responded to the "high class" woman by saying, "That's all right, Mrs. Hamer with no-long-gown-on is there, and you and I, with our long gowns, are here, and not there."[4] How easy is it for us to confuse style with substance.

Many people keep up with the latest style in cars, clothes, and commodities seeking to impress others, but having all of that does not indicate that there is any substance or purpose to their life. It is vital that you live within your means. A general rule for you should be if you can't pay cash for most of what you want, that might be a sign that you can't afford it. Now paying cash for a home or car may be impossible for you, but if you must borrow, learn to pay off debt quickly. The longer the term of the debt, the more interest you pay. Remember what scripture tells us in Proverbs 22:7, *The borrower is servant to the lender* (NIV). Pray that God will teach you to be satisfied with where you are, and know that it is always better in the long run to save than to spend. Don't let the spirit of competition lead you into a wrong relationship with money.

EXCESSIVE DESIRES

Excessive desires are different from the spirit of competition. Whereas with the spirit of competition, a person is spending to impress others, excessive desires lead us to spend to try to find satisfaction with our lives. This is not about money; this is more about a feeling of inadequacy that a person tries to fix with material things.

I was speaking to a minister friend of mine, and he said something that struck me. He said, "Don't let the failures in other areas of your life lead to desires for things that you really don't need." Desire, in itself, is not a bad thing. *Excessive* desire, however, is really about having more than enough and still wanting more. While the Bible is clear about children of God having a right to prosper and be blessed, if you really take an assessment of what you have, if you do a personal inventory of your belongings, what you may discover is that there is already more than enough.

In retrospect, did you really need another pair of shoes? Did you really need another suit or dress? Did you really need another car, another beach home, another condo that you can only visit once a year? Please do not get me wrong, I believe that we should take pleasure in having nice things as they are

Excessive desires are directly related to greed

gifts from God, but be careful that you don't start excessively desiring them, just for the sake of having them with no intended purpose. Excessive desires are directly related to greed, and greed desires more than need. Excessive desires will always lead to a wrong relationship with money.

REBELLION TO ACCOUNTABILITY

Many people have a bad relationship with money because they do not practice first-rate accountability. There is a popular theology preached in many of our churches, which is centered around the idea that the people of God have favor. Favor, in this context, simply means that a person who has faith in God, also enjoys a certain prejudice from God. It is the belief that God has given His promises to the individual because of their faith, and He will fulfill those promises, upon their time of need. There are many people today who are indeed favored by God. However, a person who has favor, but who does not understand that with that favor also comes responsibility, is really no more than a "favor fool." A "favor fool" is someone who understands favor, but does not understand obligation. Accountability is really about obligation.

Being accountable means that you know how to abide by the agreements that you make. It does not speak well for Christians to bear the name of Christ, but have financial portfolios that do not represent this truth. It does not speak well to the faith for you to have on your checks, "Jesus Is Savior," or "Too Blessed to Be Stressed," only to have these checks be returned for insufficient funds. It does not speak well for Christians to have their cars, homes, and other property repossessed because they failed to make the payments they promised to make.

I know there are people who, due to no fault of their own, lost their property in the economic downfall. This message is not for them. No, a rebellion against accountability is manifested in people who make a habit of not abiding by contracts, agreements, or payment schedules. There is a penalty to be paid for paying things late or behind schedule. It is possible that you may forfeit the opportunity to be approved for a mortgage because you turned a video in 90 days late at a video store. Would it not be a shame to be denied a home loan because of your failure to faithfully return a video that cost less than $35.00? This would be a huge misfortune!

Be accountable—pay your tithes, pay your taxes, pay your bills, pay people back the money that you owe. Honor your obligations and contracts. Maintain your favor, don't be a fool. Give an accurate representation of God by being accountable.

> *Maintain your favor, don't be a fool.*

How Do You Make a Wrong Financial Relationship Right?

David was wealthy and he was financially wise. He was wise enough to have money to take care of his obligations while he was alive, and wise enough to have resources to pass down to his son, the next generation. It was Solomon who became the heir of the wealth that David had. Solomon was the perfect choice of heir because he, too, possessed wisdom to interpret what he believed God desired for the moment.

David's son, Solomon, wrote the Book of Ecclesiastes. In this book he unfolds for us the importance of linking wisdom with finances when he declares in the seventh chapter, *Wisdom is good with an inheritance: and by it there is profit to them that see the sun. For wisdom is a defence , and money is a defence: but the Excellency of knowledge is, that wisdom giveth life to them that have it* (Ecclesiastes 7:11-12).

In the 11th chapter of Ecclesiastes, Solomon further clarifies his exposition of the importance of wisdom in finance as he unfolds practical advice for making a wrong financial relationship right.

> *Cast thy bread upon the waters: for thou shalt find it after many days. Give a portion to seven, and also to eight; for thou knowest not what evil shall be upon the earth. If the clouds be full of rain, they empty themselves upon the earth: and if the tree falls toward the south, or toward the north, in the place where the tree falleth, there it shall be. He that observeth the wind shall not sow; and he that regardeth the clouds shall not reap. As thou knowest not what is the way of the spirit, nor how the bones do grow in the womb of her that is with child: even so thou knowest not the works of God who maketh all. In the morning sow thy seed, and in the evening withhold not thine hand: for thou knowest not whether*

shall prosper either this or that, or whether they both shall be alike good.

Ecclesiastes 11:1-6

Wrap Your Money with the Word

Cast thy bread upon the waters...

The wisdom that Solomon provides in this scripture hearkens back to a time when those who were sowing seed would wait until the Nile River would rise almost to flood level. The sower would then wrap a piece of bread around the seed, and then toss the bread with the seed inside upon the waters. Eastern bread of this region most often takes the form of cakes, and it is thin so that when thrown into the water, it remains on the surface like a chip of wood, until the water permeates the cake and it descends under the water where it eventually merges into the muddy ground. The flow of the stream would carry this packet of bread encased seed much farther than the sower could toss it, thus expanding the territory from which the harvest would grow.

In making a wrong financial relationship right, it is important that you make certain that your money (seed) is wrapped tightly with the Word of God. The Word is our bread, and making certain that our money is wrapped with the Word ensures that our money is covered by the proclamations and promises that God has already made. For instance, God promises in Genesis 12:2 that He will make Abraham and his descendants (which includes you if you have accepted Christ) into a great nation. He promises to bless you and make your name great, so that you will be a blessing. God promises you in Deuteronomy 15:10, that when you give to Him freely, and not grudgingly, the Lord your God will bless you in all your work and in all that you undertake. Deuteronomy 28:13 promises, *And the LORD shall make thee the head, and not the tail; and thou shalt be above only, and thou shalt not be beneath; if that thou hearken unto the commandments of the LORD thy God, which I command thee this day, to observe and to do them.* These and other promises are yours for the claiming when you are careful to wrap your money in the Word.

Wrapping your money with the Word will also keep you from spending money on things that do not edify God or the body. It is hard to gamble money that you have wrapped with God's Word. It is not easy to expend money in clubs and bars, when you have made a vow to God that you will honor Him with the finances that He has allowed you to earn.

When your money is wrapped in the Bread, it goes further.

Wrapping your money in the Word also separates your money from the drug dealer's money, from the pimp's money, and from the gangster's money. They have money, but their money does not have the blessing of God. When your money is wrapped in the Bread, it goes further. God has a way of stretching your resources so that even if there is more month than money, God will take the little seed (money) you have and He will multiply it to make a way.

Look for the Harvest After the Flood

For thou shalt find it after many days…

Making a wrong financial relationship right, is something that will take time. The financial mess that you have created for yourself did not happen overnight, and it will not be corrected overnight. The words from Ecclesiastes 11, …*thou shalt find it after many days*, speak to the time when the flood waters would recede from the Nile River. It was then that the sower would discover where the seed had been planted. It would take many days before the sower could actually see where the seed was sown because of the flood, but when the flood subsided, he would expect to see the sprouting of a harvest. The same can be true for you when you cast your bread-wrapped seed upon the waters.

The best example I can share of this is, one day I stopped by a restaurant to grab lunch. After I placed my order and sat in my seat, a young man from across the room recognized me, and stopped filling out his job application to come over to speak to me. He informed me that he had visited my church about a month prior, and he stated how much he enjoyed the preaching and teaching. Though he wasn't a member of our church, he still found it necessary to sew financial seed into our ministry to help with our mission to transform the community.

While the young man was talking to me, the manger who was going to interview him came out, and she, too, recognized me. I did not recognize either one of them. All I knew was that this young man who had been to my church a month ago, gave money in the offering, and now he needed a job. I also knew that the person who could hire him was also standing there talking to me. So I turned and said to the manger, "Ma'am, I don't have anything to do with your hiring process, but I was talking to this young man, and my spirit says that he is a good man, and you should hire him."

Without even looking at his resume and application, she said to him, "Sir, I have never hired anyone without reviewing their application, but based on the preacher's word, you have the job." That young man yelled out in the restaurant, "Thank you, Jesus!"

This experience helped me understand what the Word meant when it said, ...*thou shalt find it after many days.* Because this young man sowed a seed into our ministry, God, in turn, compelled me to sow a seed for him. This man sowed a seed by coming to our church, by giving during the offering, by complementing the preaching and teaching, and by coming over to speak to me. Because he had been faithful to cast his bread upon the water, the Spirit moved me to sow a seed, and my seed was a word of confidence on his behalf. So after many days, 30 days to be exact, he found what he sowed. The job he was seeking, he received, all because he dared to sow.

When you sow finances, good deeds, or honorable efforts into the kingdom of God, do not expect immediate results. It takes time. Therefore, while you are sowing into the kingdom, do not be discouraged if it seems like God has you on a delay plan, actually you are right on schedule. You may have been flooded with bills, flooded with taxes, flooded with obligations, flooded with unanticipated expenses, and some of these floods may have come because of your own poor decisions, but hope is found in the knowledge that floods do subside. It takes time to really master living by a budget. It takes time to get your savings to a place where you really feel comfortable. It takes time to pay off bills that are draining you, with interest rates that are too much for you. It takes time. However, scripture declares that if you continue to sow finances, good deeds, and honorable efforts into the kingdom of God, after many days you will find your harvest. We are not always certain how it will show up, or when it will show up, but we do know that a harvest is on the way.

> *Hope is found in the knowledge that floods do subside.*

LOOK FOR A SEVEN AND AN EIGHT

Give a portion to seven, and also to eight; for thou knowest not what evil shall be upon the earth.

The number seven is the number of 'completion,' and the number eight is a number of 'new beginnings.' Solomon in his wisdom declares that financial relationships must extend to people that represent both *seven* and *eight*.

Essentially, what he is saying when he exorts you to "give a portion to seven," is that there comes a time when you should sow financial seed into people who look like they are already complete. In other words, there are times when you should actively seek out people to give to who look like they have more than you. Their car may be nicer and newer than yours, their home may be more immaculate than yours, they may even have a better job than you have or make more money than you make. Solomon says it is good to establish a relationship with people who have more than you have—who appear more "complete" than you—because when you learn to sow into their success, it is sign that you are not envious. Therefore, you are more likely to learn from them and even duplicate what they are doing to be successful. The anointing that you appreciate is the anointing that you invite into your own life. Solomon says to give to them because evil is upon the earth. Giving to the "sevens" in your life should be viewed as a means of investment, because when you give to them, when you find yourself in your own time of need because of evil in the land, they may willing to give back to you.

Likewise Solomon declares that you should also give to people who are "eights." Eight is the number of new beginnings. Solomon says that there comes a time when you should give to people who look like they are trying to begin a work, who are struggling to start something or are in the process of initiating a project. This may mean that we investing in someone who is trying to start a business, who is trying to work their way through college, or that we invest in those who are struggling to pay their bills, or even looking to establish a memorable landmark. Solomon says that it is good to invest in eights because you never know when you are going to be in need, as evil is upon the earth. Give to eights because, while today you may have a job, tomorrow you may not, and when you have invested in this way, then those you have invested in will have no problem investing in you. Give to eights because, while they may not look like they have much now, your willingness to invest your resources in them will make a difference in their life, and possibly one day, in yours.

Don't Look at the Wind, Keep Your Eyes on God

He that observeth the wind shall not sow; and he that regardeth the clouds shall not reap.

One of the things that we must do to develop a good relationship with our finances is learn how to develop confidence in what our money can accomplish. When your finances are covered by God's Word and you have a workable plan that reflects a right motive, there is no reason to attach fear to your finances.

Solomon declares that those who observe the wind shall not sow. The wind can be interpreted as turbulent times, as moments when there is great uncertainty. Americans are all too familiar with "the wind" due to the recent collapse of the American economy, with the resultant loss of many jobs and financial securities. In these turbulent times, there were many people who feared sowing into the kingdom of God and supporting the ministry as God had called them to do. There are times when God will allow turbulent winds to blow in our lives for us to prove our trust in Him. We prove our trust in Him by always paying our tithes and giving offerings, in spite of the times in which we live. Doing these things finances His campaign for blessings in our lives.

Luke 6:38, says *Give, and it shall be given unto you; good measure, pressed down, and shaken together, and running over, shall men give into your bosom. For with the same measure that ye mete withal it shall be measured to you again.*" While turbulent winds and dark clouds in our lives make us concerned about our future, our trust should rest in the fact that if we take care of God, God will take care of us.

Our trust should rest in the fact that if we take care of God, God will take care of us.

Trusting God also requires that you be a wise spender, a wise planner, a wise saver, and a wise discerner. Solomon declares that there is a time and a season for all things (Ecclesiastes 3:1), and you have to discern whether it is a good time to buy a new home, get a new car, or spend money at the mall on stuff you already have. You have to discern when it is the right time to invest and when to cash in on your investments. In all of this, keep in mind that it is always time to sow into the kingdom, regardless of your other financial obligations and responsibilities, and in spite the winds that blow and the clouds that rise.

Financial Strategies that Enhance Right Relationship

- Right relationships with finances happen when you change your attitude about money, and realize that it is a blessing from God, given so that you can be a blessing to God, others, and yourself.

- Right relationships with finances happen when you honor God faithfully and consistently with your tithes and offerings.

- Right relationships with finances happen when you evaluate your personal budget at least quarterly and make sure that you try to operate within that budget.

- Right relationships with finances happen when you save at least 5 to 10 percent for yourself after you give God His 10 percent. Planning for the future in this way can alleviate many stresses about "surprise" expenses.

- Right relationships with finances happen when you do not live beyond your means. Try this: cut your personal budget by 5 percent every year. Cutting your expenses is a way to, in essence, give yourself a pay increase.

- Right relationships with finances happen when you pay your taxes, bills, and other financial obligations on time.

Be prompt in your payments, always remembering that your character is attached to your finances.

- Right relationships with finances happen when you seek to purchase things with cash or debit card only. Get the albatross out from around your neck by eradicating credit card debt as soon as possible. Only use a credit card when it is absolutely necessary.

- Right relationships with finances happen when you work to pay at least one extra payment on your mortgage as often as possible. Doing so not only gives you a feeling of accomplishment, but it will also cut down on the years of the loan.

- Right relationships with finances happen when you investigate the best investments for your situation and your future. Do not watch the stock market daily. It will only lead to anxiety. Investments should be for long-term benefits. Be willing to be patient as you wait for good returns.

- Right relationships with finances happen when you develop good relationships with banks and financial institutions. Good relationships with banks and other financial institutions lead to the best interest rates.

- Right relationships with finances happen when you look for ways to help others, while being discerning about who you help. You do not have unlimited funds to blow, so pray about who to extend a helping hand to. Never loan money that you are not willing to give away, that way, if the borrower does not pay it back, it will not be a source of bitterness for you.

FINANCIAL RELATIONSHIP REFLECTION QUESTIONS

1. Did your parents teach you any financial principles? If so, how did their teaching help shape your understanding of finances today?

2. What are some smart things that you are doing with your finances at this point? What are some areas you need to improve?

3. What are some dreams that you have for your life, and what do you need to do financially to accomplish those dreams and desires?

4. There is a section in this chapter that mentions helping people who already have, and helping people financially who are about to establish a work. Who have you helped financially in the past? Do you think it was a good investment?

5. Most people have had to make adjustments in their financial operations because of the recent economic downturn. What adjustments have you had to make, and how have those adjustments affected your lifestyle?

6. List five things that you are going to do differently in the coming year to ensure that you will have a right relationship with your finances.

CHAPTER 11

MAKING A WRONG
Heart Relationship Right

Create in me a clean heart, O God; and renew a right spirit within me.

Psalm 51:10

One of the most familiar verses of scripture penned by David, which he wrote following his fall with Bathsheba, is found in Psalm 51:10. In this verse, David says, *Create in me a clean heart, O God; and renew a right spirit within me.* It is vital that we understand the importance of conditioning one's heart and spirit for right relationships. It is fitting that this would be the final chapter of this book on relationships, because for any relationship to be effective, it is most important that the heart is right.

In this verse, we find David coming to a moment of conclusion about all of the relationships he had experienced. Every life must have a moment of conclusion. That is the moment when you collectively evaluate the experiences that bring you to a certain point. It is when you get to the place where you do the addition, subtraction, multiplication, and division with the relationship experiences that you have had, and then you make a conclusion about how those relationships have impacted you and shaped you to where you presently are.

In the introduction of this book, I talked about pre-relationships, practicing relationships, and post-relationships. You will remember that *pre-relationships* include those experiences in the journey that we take prior to developing a relationship with someone else. For an example, if you were to meet a person that you have interest in, more than likely your discussion on the first date would be about your experiences prior to both of you meeting.

Practicing relationships include the things that we do in the relationships. Remember, most of what we do in the practicing relationship is often shaped by the things that we witnessed and experienced in our pre-relationships. Using the same example about the budding relationship, after the two of you meet and discuss life prior to your meeting, you now take those pre-relationship exposures and begin to develop the relationship between the two of you. This is the practicing relationship.

Post-relationships refer to who we become as a result of the relationships that we have been involved in. Every relationship makes deposits in our lives, and every relationship someday will end. Even though a relationship is no longer active in our life, there is residue that we still hold on to, and this moves us to a post-relationship.

I believe David considered His relationship with God from a pre-, practicing, and post- perspective. In taking inventory of his relationship with God from each of these perspectives, David comes to his moment of conclusion. David realizes that something has happened to de-rail his relationship with God, and he realizes that the relationship is in need of restoration.

Upon coming to this moment of conclusion, David declares in Psalm 51:7-13:

> *Purge me with hyssop, and I shall be clean: wash me, and I shall be whiter than snow. Make me to hear joy and gladness; that the bones which thou hast broken may rejoice. Hide thy face from my sins, and blot out all mine iniquities. Create in me a clean heart, O God; and renew a right spirit within me. Cast me not away from thy presence; and take not thy holy spirit from me. Restore unto me the joy of thy salvation; and uphold me with thy free spirit. Then will I teach transgressors thy ways; and sinners shall be converted unto thee.*

After David talks about being purged, washed, revived in his bones, and having his sins washed away, David then says, *Create in me a clean heart.* It is the heart moment that caught my attention, because I remembered how often David was referred to as a man after God's own heart. God looked to the heart of David when He was looking to replace the evil heart of Saul. Remember the scene when Samuel had come to the home of David's father, Jesse. (See 1 Samuel 16.) All of the sons of Jesse were brought before Samuel, but God did not allow Samuel to select Saul's replacement based off of looks or seniority. God led Samuel to choose David because of David's heart. David's pre-relationship with God prior to his fall with Bathsheba, the murder of Uriah, and the drama between his two sons Amnon and Absalom, was marked by the purity that he had in his heart. God did find a good-looking warrior in David, but He most desired a warrior who had a heart like His.

This reminds me of the novel entitled *Searching for David's Heart*, written by Cherie Bennett.[1] In that book Darcy Deeton is a twelve-year-old girl who loves her older brother, David. After becoming jealous when he falls in love with a girl by the name of Jayne Evans, Darcy leads David to his death in a car accident. The parents decided to donate David's most important organ, his heart. Darcy's life is so filled with guilt that she embarks upon an adventurous journey to find the one person who has her brother's heart. There is a parallel here between Darcy's search and God's search. God does not embark on His search out of guilt, as Darcy does, but both are searching for a heart with certain desirable characteristics. This search Darcy embarks upon is most intriguing because it is something that we all should do, actually. We should be searching within ourselves to have a heart with characteristics God desires. This is what God is searching for and what we should be searching for as well. Is our heart full of righteousness, holiness, love, and peace?

Right Heart in the Pre-

Having a right heart in the pre-relationship stage is important because it keeps us from doing things that can be detrimental to our future relationships. It takes great wisdom and insight to realize that every opportunity we are presented is an opportunity to prepare for the future relationships that God will bring into our lives. Therefore, it behooves us to make wise choices and do all we can to avoid situations that will haunt us for the rest of our lives. We have to prepare for future relationships that are destined to come our way.

Right Heart in the Practicing

A right heart in a practicing relationship will keep all motives clear and honest. In this stage of relationship, a right heart helps us to understand that we must give our best and be determined not settle for less than excellence from others. A right heart in a practicing relationship helps us with giving and forgiving, being selfless and sanctified, transparent and truthful, useful and understanding. A right heart seeks to do right at all times, so that there won't be so many times when apologies are needed, resignations received, and explanations expressed.

Right Heart in the Post-

A right heart start will, most of the time, lead to a right heart end. Never underestimate the importance of a right heart in the post-relationship, with relationships that are no longer active in our lives. Relationships end for various and sundry reasons, and we can't always predict or even control how they will end. However, we can control whether our heart is right when they do end. A right heart at this *post* stage will help you heal, overcome, sustain, release, and be stabilized in the place where God has you after a relationship is over.

David was taking a retrospective look at his heart, when he noticed that his heart was right in the pre-relationship, but then something happened to his heart in the practicing. Now in the post-relationship state, he is coming to the realization that no other relationships matter to him but his relationship with God. Upon this realization, he prays a prayer, asking God to, *Create in me a clean heart, O God; and renew a right spirit within me* (Psalm 51:10). David was reflecting on the sin that drove a wedge in his relationship with God and the state of that relationship grieved him. David came to a breaking point—he realized that even with all of the money that he had, with all of the power that he possessed, with all of the influence that he had, with all of the authority that was bestowed upon him, he didn't have the power to make his own heart right. So he cries out, putting his reliance solely on God, knowing that only God could give him a clean heart and a right spirit.

The Benefits of Having a Right Heart

Recently, there was a story that made headline news that offered itself to the world as a modern day miracle. It was the story about an 11-year-old girl by the name of Nadia, who was missing in a Florida swamp for several days. While there were rescue teams, hunting dogs, and public safety officials with heat detectors searching four days for Nadia, God had another plan for her to be found.

It all began when a man by the name of James King went searching for Nadia independent from the search teams. James King decided that this little girl's life was too valuable to leave in a swamp without giving his best effort to find her, so he packed lunches for him and for Nadia, thinking that, in the event that he found her, he could offer her food. James loaded up his bag and made his way to the swamp areas to search for Nadia.

Not only did James King have the right heart to search for a girl who had no personal attachment to him, but James King was also a man who had a right heart for God. James was not only in the swamp searching, but this man was also in the swamp praying. In the midst of his prayers, James King says that God spoke to him and told him early one morning to just start walking towards the sun. He walked to a certain point and began to yell Nadia's name. To his surprise, Nadia answered by simply saying, "Yes." James King went over to where he heard the voice and there was Nadia, sitting up against a tree in a swamp. He took the lunch out of his bag, and began to feed Nadia, and then called for the rescue team. The rescue team located James and Nadia and returned the girl back to her family and to a place of safety.

It is in this most celebrative moment, the world was able to witness a real miracle. Consider these reasons why I would suggest that this was more than mere coincidence, but rather it was more "God-cidence" as He worked through a willing person with a heart like His.

A RIGHT HEART MEANS HAVING A RIGHT WORD

God didn't just send a man named James King, but he sent a man who had the King James Bible in his bag and in his heart. This is not to put emphasis on what translation of the Bible this man had with him, but what was key was that he had the Word of God in his bag and in his heart.

What a powerful message for all of us! How many of us go out to seek the lost without having God's Word with us in our bags or in our hearts? It is critical that we keep the Word of God near us, and more importantly, that it be within our hearts. Psalm 119:11 says, *Thy word have I hid in mine heart, that I might not sin against thee.* Having a right heart, means that the Word is hidden in your heart.

Having a right heart, means that the Word is hidden in your heart.

When you find yourself in a situation that may be trying in your life, the Word in your heart will minister to you. Keep that Word in your heart which says, *All things work together for good to them that love God, to them who are the called according to his purpose* (Romans 8:28).

Keep the Word in your heart which says in 2 Corinthians 4:17, *For our light affliction, which is but for a moment, worketh for us a far more exceeding and eternal weight of glory.* Keep the Word in your heart which encourages you in this way, *Therefore if any man be in Christ, he is a new creature: old things are passed away; behold, all things are become new* (2 Corinthians 5:17).

A Right Heart Is Moving in the Right Direction

James King said the Lord spoke to him and told him to move towards the sun. God has His own GPS system and it never fails. When James King went in the direction God sent him and called that little girl's name, she answered and was found.

Whenever our heart moves towards the SON, we, too, can call and Jesus will answer. Moving in the right direction means always moving towards the way of Christ. *There is a way that seemeth right unto a man, but the end thereof are the ways of death* (Proverbs 16:25). Right direction living begins by having a heart that is willing to hear what God is speaking. Not only must our heart hear, but it must also be willing to respond to what is being spoken.

> *Moving in the right direction means always moving towards the way of Christ.*

Recently, I had the opportunity to meet and have my picture taken with the First Lady of the United States of America, Michelle Obama. While I was in awe just to be standing next to Mrs. Obama, I felt most honored when I shook her hand, spoke to her, and she took the time to speak back to me. I was excited and considered it a great honor to have Michelle Obama speak to me. I told my family Michelle Obama spoke to me, I told my church that Michelle Obama spoke to me. Now if I got that excited about Michelle Obama speaking to me, what do you think happens in my spirit when God speaks to me? Not only is God willing to speak to me, but if you give him a chance He will speak to you!

A Right Heart Relationship Is when You Prepare to Find What You Are Looking For

When God speaks a word into your heart and gives you a promise to hold on to, a right heart knows how to prepare for what God has promised. James King saw a miracle because he prepared for one. It is not recorded if anybody else in the rescue teams prepared for a miracle before the search, but James King did. Interviewers asked him what he prepared for Nadia to eat. King said, "I brought an apple, a green apple, and I brought her a nutritional shake because I knew she'd be dehydrated and wouldn't have eaten in some time." This man prepared to find the miracle he was looking for.

A right heart knows how to prepare to receive what God has promised. Consider God's promise an engagement ring on your destiny. The engagement ring is a sign for everybody to see to let them know that they can expect a wedding real soon. The wedding is on the way, so go ahead and get the gown, get the tux, order the cake, send the invitations, call the photographer, and tell the preacher to prepare the vows. In your life, the wedding of joy, the wedding of peace, the wedding of prosperity, the wedding of good health, the wedding of promotion, the wedding of power, and the wedding of a miracle is on the way. In your heart, prepare for what God has already promised you will find. Matthew 7:7 reminds us, *Ask and it shall be given you; seek, and ye shall find; knock, and it shall be opened unto you.*

A RIGHT HEART WILL GO INTO A SWAMP TO FIND WHAT IT IS LOOKING FOR, IF IT HAS TO

The miracle is not that this girl was found in a swamp, but the miracle is this man was willing to go into the swamp to find her. A swamp is a low-lying wetland of deep, soft soil or mud that sinks underfoot with large algae covering the water's surface. It's easy to sink in a swamp. Figuratively speaking, there are many people who are in swamps today. There are many people who are in situations where they are sinking and cannot stand.

A person in a swamp lives below God's standards, hooked on drugs, addicted to alcohol, prostituting their body, living with a partner without being married. A person in a swamp has a marriage that is in shambles, lives in a relationship where they have lost themselves, or lives life thinking it is all about them. Swamp living is being comfortable with the lifestyle of cursing, homosexuality, lesbianism, fornication and adultery. Swamp living leaves you where you can't stand because so many people keep knocking you down. Your circumstances are like quicksand that keeps pulling you down deeper and deeper. You are sunk so deep in your swamp, that the only way out is by somebody else pulling you out.

If you are reading this book, you have spent some time in the swamp. You may not have been guilty of any of those wrong relationships I specifically mentioned, but you have been in a swamp called sin. God tells us in Romans 3:23, *For all have sinned, and come short of the glory of God.* Because we all sinned and were lost in those sins, God sent His only Son to come and find us in our swamp.

When God sent Jesus to the swamp to find us, people in the swamp sought to kill Him. While trying to rescue us from our swamp of sin, He did die a brutal death. Jim Bishop in his book, "The Day That Christ Died,"[2] records all of the physical trauma that Jesus was subjected to as He paid the price to save us while we were in the swamp of sin. They marched Him up that 650-yard journey from the Fortress Antonia to the place called Golgotha Hill. On Friday, they put a 110 pound splintered cross upon His back, and when He stumbled, they compelled a North African black man named Simon of Cyrene, with dread locks in his hair and muscles to bear, to help Jesus carry the cross. On Friday, they put the crown of thorns on His head, and they put the nails in His wrist and nails in His feet. With His body slowly sagging down, the nails in His wrist caused a fiery pain that shot along the fingers, up the arms, causing excruciating pain. The nails in His wrist put pressure on the median nerve, until his hand began to involuntarily take the shape of a claw. In the words of Bishop Noel Jones, it was as if Christ Jesus had a death grip on sin.

On that Friday, the arms of Jesus became fatigued as He hung on the cross, and cramps set in His muscles. His pectoral chest muscles were paralyzed, and the intercostal muscles between His ribs were unable to function. Now carbon dioxide levels increased in His lungs and throughout His blood stream. As He gasped for breath on the cross, between these breaths He uttered words like, *Father, forgive them; for they know not what they do* (Luke 23:34), *Father, into thy hands I commend my spirit* (Luke 23:46), and *It is finished* (John 19:30). As He hung on the cross, enduring the agony, He reached way down and pulled us out of our swamp.

Jesus Christ died to save us from our swamp.

Jesus Christ died to save us from our swamp. But remember, Jesus said it was finished, He didn't say He was finished. Early Sunday morning, He got up with all power in heaven and on earth in His hand. It was with those hands that He reached out to save you, to pull you out of your swamp and deliver you into your miracle. Jesus Christ was willing to go into the swamp to rescue you, to deliver you into the destiny He prepared for you.

Regardless of what relationship you may have had that turned from right to wrong to land you in a swamp, the good news is that if you put your heart and your trust in the Lord, He is able to pull you and your relationship out. He's in the business of making wrong relationships right.

HEART RELATIONSHIP REFLECTION QUESTIONS

1. What are some things that happened in your life that gave you the desire to have a heart for God?

2. What pre-relationship heart wounds have you suffered that affected you in a practicing relationship later on?

3. What are some disciplines you can practice that will help you become more committed to God and the call that He has on your life?

4. When is the best time for you to meditate and worship God privately? What benefits have you noticed from committing to do this?

5. Thinking about the story about James King finding Nadia in a swamp, when can you recall God leading you to do something and as a result, you found what you were looking for?

6. How do you plan on helping others develop a right heart relationship with God?

ENDNOTES

Introduction

[1] Gardner C. Taylor, *The Words of Gardner Taylor: Volume 2, Sermons from the Middle Years 1970-1980* (Valley Forge: Judson Press, 2000), 51.

Chapter 1

[1] Greg Easterbrook, *The Progress Paradox* (New York: Random House, 2004), 39.

[2] Vern Mclellan, *Timeless Treasures* (Peabody: Hendrickson Publishers Inc, 2000), 107.

[3] Benjamin Mays, *Quotable Quotes of Benjamin E. Mays* (New York: Vantage Press, Inc., 1983), 3.

[4] Henri J. M. Nouwen, *Sabbatical Journey: The Diary of His Final Year* (New York: Crossroad Publishing, 2000), 81-82.

Chapter 2

[1] Howard Gardner, *Leading Minds: An Anatomy of Leadership* (New York: Basic Books, The Perseus Books Group, 1995), ix.

[2] Ronald A. Heifetz and Martin Linsky, *Leadership On The Line: Staying Alive Through the Dangers of Leading* (Boston: Harvard Business School Press, 2002), 2.

[3] Bill Hull, *7 Steps To Transform Your Church* (Grand Rapids: Baker Book House, 1997), 39.

[4] Walter Earl Fluker, *Ethical Leadership-The Quest for Character, Civility, and Community* (Minneapolis: Fortress Press), 66.

[5] Roy B. Zuck, *The Speaker's Quote Book* (Grand Rapids: Kregal Publications, 1997), 212.

[6] Vernon McLellan, *Timeless Treasures: Classic Quotations for Speaking, Writing and Teaching* (Peabody, Massachusetts: Hendrickson Publishers, 2000), 33.

[7] James M. Gustafson, *Christ and the Moral Life* (Chicago and London: Chicago University Press, 1968), 250.

Chapter 3

[1] Larry Burkett, *The Complete Guide To Managing Your Money*, (New York: Inspirational Press, 1993), 271.

[2] ibid, 273.

[3] Rick Ezell, *The Seven Sins of Highly Defective People*, (Grand Rapids: Kregel Publications, 2003).

[4] Frederick Buechner, *Godric: A Novel*, (San Francisco: HarperSanFrancisco, 1980), 143.

[5] Rick Ezell, *The Seven Sins of Highly Defective People*, (Grand Rapids: Kregel Publications, 2003), 35.

[6] ibid, 70-71.

[7] David Pauley, "True Greed: The Downfall of Ivan Boesky," *Newsweek*, December 1, 1986, 48.

Chapter 4

[1] Plato, *Symposium*. Translated by Alexander Nehamas and Paul Woodruff (Indianapolis: Hackett Publishing Co., 1989), 25.

[2] Thomas Moore, "Soulmate Quotes" JoyofQuotes.com. http://www.joyofquotes.com/soulmate_quotes.html (accessed June 3, 2010).

Chapter 6

[1] Ovid, *Ovid: Metamorphoses Books 1-8*. Edited by G.P. Goold, Translated by Frank Justis Miller (Suffolk : St. Edmundsbury Press, Ltd., 1916)

Chapter 7

[1] H.D.M. Spence-Jones and Joseph Exell, editors. *The Pulpit Commentary: 2 Samuel* (Bellingham, Washington : Logos Research Systems, Inc., 2004).

[2] Thom Geier et al. 2009. "100 Greatest Movies, TV Shows, and More." http://www.ew.com/ew/article/0,,20324138,00.html (accessed June 5, 2010.)

[3] Simon McGregor-Wood, 2010. "Facebook Details Force Israeli Military to Cancel Operation." http://abcnews.go.com/International/facebook-details-force-israeli-military-cancel-operation/story?id=10006343 (accessed June 7, 2010.)

[4] M.P. McQueen, 2009. "Bloggers, Beware: What You Write Can Get You Sued." http://online.wsj.com/article/SB124287328648142113.html (accessed June 7, 2010.)

[5] Michael O'Brien, 2009. "Obama Open to Newspaper Bailout Bill." http://thehill.com/blogs/blog-briefing-room/news/59523-obama-open-to-newspaper-bailout-bill (accessed June 7, 2010.)

Chapter 8

[1] Lee N. June and Sabrina D. Black, editors, *Counseling in African-American Communities* (Grand Rapids : Zondervan, 2002) 36.

[2] G. Lloyd Carr, *The Song of Solomon: An Introduction and Commentary* (Tyndale Old Testament Commentaries) (Downers Grove : InterVarsity, 1984) Song 2:8-3:5.

[3] ibid.

[4] James Strong, *Strong's Exhaustive Concordance to the Bible* (Peabody: Hendrickson Publishers Inc., 2009)

[5] Lee McGlone, editor, *The Mininsters Manual, 2009 Edition* (San Francisco : Jossey Bass, A Wiley Imprint, 2008) 464.

[6] Willie Richardson, *Reclaiming the Urban Family* (Grand Rapids : Zondervan Publishing House, 1996), 94-100.

[7] ibid, 97.

[8] ibid, 88.

[9] ibid, 106.

Chapter 9

[1] Gabi Köpp, *Warum war ich bloss ein Mädchen?* (Germany : Herbig Auflage, 2010).

[2] Iyanla Vanzant, *Acts of Faith: Daily Meditations for People of Color* (New York : Fireside, 1993), September 9.

Chapter 10

[1] Wallace Witkowski, 2010. "Carlos Slim Helu named world's richest by Forbes." http://www.marketwatch.com/story/carlos-sim-helu-named-worlds-richest-by-forbes-2010-03-10 (accessed June 10, 2010.)

[2] Brainy Quote, http://www.brainyquote.com/quotes/authors/g/george_horace_lorimer.html (accessed June 29, 2010).

[3] Kelvin Boston, *Smart Money Moves For African Americans* (New York : G.P. Putnam & Sons Publishers, 1996), 205-211.

[4] Marion Wright Edelman, "Children's Defense Fund, An Agenda For Empowerment" *Essence*, May 1988, 133.

Chapter 11

[1] Cherie Bennett, *Searching for David's Heart: A Christmas Story* (New York : Scholastic, 1998).

[2] Jim Bishop, *The Day Christ Died* (New York : Harper, 1957).

ABOUT THE AUTHOR

Reverend Dr. Sir Walter L. Mack Jr. is pastor and teacher of the 4,000 member Union Baptist Church in Winston-Salem, North Carolina, where a street was recently named in his honor. His ministry finds strength nationally and internationally with progressive ministry programs like the Corner to Corner Street Life Conference, a conference designed to transform the lives of drug dealers and drug users. Dr. Mack is the organizer and founder of the Character Football League, a league designed to enhance behavior and lifestyle choices of young people. Dr. Mack has participated in programs at various colleges and universities including Harvard University and Oxford University in Oxford, England. Mack was cited as one of the top 20 preachers to watch under 40 by the African American Pulpit Journal. Dr. Mack is the author of other publications such as, *Passion for Your Kingdom Purpose*, *Destined for Promotion*, and *Hope for Hip Hop*. For more information on Dr. Mack, visit www.unionbaptistwsnc.org